To: MIKE

Enjoy my book!

Best Regards.

R. Kent Morgan   9/14/04

Our Hallowed Ground

Guide To Indian War Battlefield Locations in Eastern Montana

By

R. KENT MORGAN

authorHOUSE

1663 LIBERTY DRIVE, SUITE 200
BLOOMINGTON, INDIANA 47403
(800) 839-8640
www.authorhouse.com

First published by AuthorHouse 05/25/04

ISBN: 1-4184-0472-1 (e)
ISBN: 1-4184-0473-X (sc)

Library of Congress Control Number: 2004093440

Printed in the United States of America
Bloomington, Indiana

This book is printed on acid-free paper.

This book is dedicated with affection to my wife, Linda,
my sons, John, Richard, my daughter Christie,
my daughter-in-law Cindy, my son-in-law Dionne,
my grandson Jesse and my granddaughter Kate

In Memorial to
Gary Larsen and Lester Jens

Table of Contents

Preface

This Guide Book was written for those who are interested in touring the battlefields and forts of the American Indian Wars in eastern Montana. The reason these Indian Campaigns were fought was political: a growing need for expansion (Manifest Dynasty) after the Civil War, the discovery of gold and the vision of connecting the east and west coast together via the railroad. There are several books that discuss the political issues that lead to the Indian Wars. To enrich your experience and adventure, I have included the locations of specific sites.

One should carry some basic items that will be extremely helpful:
1)   Current Montana road map
2)   Common compass
3)   Binoculars

Optional items:
1)   Handheld GPS (some rental cars have a GPS feature)
2)   Camera

This book gives you battlefield locations via GPS coordinates (for isolated battlefield sites), compass headings, maps and driving directions to the most advantageous viewing points, conditions of roads leading to them, as well as some points of interest along the way.

To get an idea of which battlefields are closest and their locations, I would suggest looking at a Montana State Map to determine where you will begin your battlefield "tour". Then you can plan your adventure accordingly, depending upon where in Montana you begin.

How you map your journey is up to you, the reader, but I have it laid out in the following sequence by chapter:

If you follow this route on a Montana State map, it forms a large triangle. From Billings, take I-94 to Pompey's Pillar, then on to Custer, Miles City, Terry, Glendive and Fort Buford. Backtrack from there to Miles City, south to Broadus, west to Lame Deer, south again to Birney and Rosebud Battlefield, west to Little Big Horn Battlefield and Harden, then on to Fort C.F. Smith, then Chief Plenty Coups State Park, Laurel and back to Billings.

Chapters are set up according to the name of the battlefield, fort or cantonment, with locations and driving directions (with or without GPS position), and include a brief history, current pictures of the sites, the campaign name, pertinent date(s), principal commanders involved, forces engaged, estimated casualties, and Medal of Honor recipients. There were 428 Medals of Honor awarded during the Indian War campaigns. This is twenty two percent of the total medals awarded since the Civil War. Please refer to **Appendix # 1** for an explanation.

Also included are additional points of interest with their GPS positions, and other bits of information and trivia I have gathered while actually visiting these sites and interviewing ranch owners.

It has always been interesting to learn what happened to these soldiers subsequent to the Indian Wars. Where did their careers take them? What rank did they achieve at retirement? Where are they buried? **Appendix # 2** contains several soldiers' biographies.

Several history books and articles reference the Indian Treaty of 1868, also known by its official name *The Fort Laramie Treaty of 1868*. The full text is included in **Appendix # 3**.

In **Appendix # 4** is a brief on the creation of the *Indian Campaign Medal*, authorized by Congress some 42 years after the Indian Wars began.

The Indian War Campaigns are located in a reasonably small area of Eastern Montana, and easily driven to plus toured on foot with some basic preplanning. All battlefield sites can be visited in five or six days. Most of the following battlefield sites are almost exactly as they were back in 1876 and 1877, except for some natural soil erosion.

The Little Bighorn and Rosebud sites are much as they were save for a road which now runs through them. While the Little Bighorn is the most developed, the Rosebud has remained mostly in its original state. While the Rosebud site is not as developed as Little Bighorn, it certainly can easily be walked. If you wish to drive through, there is a dirt road that winds through the battlefield which provides excellent views of all major points of the battle.

Wolf Mountain Battlefield is now farmland, from the Tongue River to the westernmost of two buttes. A gravel road dissects the buttes, which are only 200 yards apart. The buttes are in their natural state.

Lame Deer's Village Site is now residential, however, the retreat route area remains in its natural state. The Powder River, Cedar Creek and Ash Creek sites remain as they were when fought over. Some of the Cedar Creek Battlefield is public land under the Bureau of Land Management, and can be walked on the north side of the fence line. The National Park Service oversees the Little Bighorn. Where Rosebud battlefield is a Montana State Park. The remaining sites noted in this guidebook are privately owned.

At the Rosebud site there are signs at the entrance and an excellent brochure is available, with pictures denoting the progress of the battle.

On a Montana State map, find Hardin, on I-90. Twelve miles south of Hardin you will find the Little Bighorn Battlefield.

At the Little Bighorn there are several points of interest. These include the Museum, the National Cemetery, Last Stand Hill, Indian Memorial, Weir's Point, Medicine Tail Coulee, and the Reno/Benteen Defense Point. All sites are connected by blacktop road. Major Reno's first attack on the eastern end of the village lay on both sides of what is now the I-90 freeway, and very close to the Gerryowen Trading Post.

On the southeast portion of your map, you will find the Rosebud Battlefield near Decker. Veer northeast a bit to find Birney, which is located near Wolf Mountain Battlefield. Further north, on U.S. Route 212, is the site of the Lame Deer Fight in the town of Lame Deer.

Continue to search Route 212 for Broadus. South of Broadus on County Road 391 is the Powder River Battlefield.

From Broadus, look north on U.S. Route 59 to Miles City on I-94; here you will find Fort Keogh and the Tongue River Cantonment, just off the highway.

From Miles City follow I-94 to Terry, then north on U.S. Route 253 to the Cedar Creek Road on your right, where you will find the Cedar Creek Battlefield. Four miles north of Cedar Creek is the Ash Creek Battlefield.

From Terry, go east on I-94 to U.S. Route 16 for Glendive Cantonment and continue north to Fort Buford and Fort Union.

Note: All battles were fought near a creek or river, for example, Little Bighorn, Rosebud, Tongue, and Powder are rivers south of the

Yellowstone River. Cedar Creek and Ash Creek (also called Red Water Creek) lay to the north of it. These were all grazing areas to which buffalo migrated; the Indians followed this essential food source.

A ranger at Pompey's Pillar said that the Indians called the Yellowstone River "Elk River". Lewis and Clark had noted the abundance of elk herds that lived around the river. Clark also noted he had to wait some 2 1/2 hours for thousands of Buffalo to cross the Yellowstone River at Glendive (just off I-94).

Clark perhaps had to wait on a herd crossing at Pompey's Pillar when he carved his name into the Sandstone Pillar, named after Sacagewea's young son Pompey. You can visit this site just 31 miles northeast from Billings on I-94.

Driving from one area to another in eastern Montana is very enjoyable- there is a variety of beautiful scenery: rolling prairie, awesome rock formations and wonderful wildlife, especially deer and antelope that abounds on the prairie.

NOTE: Please be EXTREMELY cautious of wildlife when driving at night. My recommendation is to drive after dawn to dusk, even on the major freeways. If you think this is a joke, you need only count the number of dead deer on the sides of the roads. Due to mild winters the last few years, the deer population has grown immensely. Please use caution.

Another area of concern while driving is the county gravel roads. Although quite dusty, these roads are normally quite good. Use caution when driving over rises, stay on the right side of the road for local traffic and don't drive too fast for the road.

I would like to recognize several generous people who have inspired, encouraged, mentored, shared information, guided, and allowed me access to these various battlefields and fort sites: The late Lester Jens, Former Director of Prairie County Historical Society, Terry, MT;

Adele Jens, Terry, MT; the late Gary Larsen, Director of Prairie County Historical Society, Terry, MT; Carol Larsen, Terry, MT; The Volunteer Staff of Prairie County Historical Society, Terry, MT; Lorin Larsen, Terry, MT; Jerry and Barb Smalis, Terry, MT; Walter Stepper, Terry, MT; the late Charles Grue, Terry, MT; Clint and Sandra Grue, Terry, MT; Bob and Betty Barthelmess, Directors of Range Riders Museum, Miles City, MT; Bureau of Land Management, Miles City, MT; Putt and Jill Thompson, Crow Agency, MT; David Kasten, Brockway, MT; Jack and Carol Bailey, Forsyth, MT; Gary and Elsie Cunningham, Hysham, MT; and Stacey and Tiffany Ogren, Hysham, MT; Kathy Iverson, Monroe, WA; Diane Nicks, Lake Stevens, WA; Becky Haney, Everett, WA; Mark and Carol Morgan, Leesburg, FL; Martha V. Morgan, Beardstown, IL; Freddy A. Morgan, Beardstown, IL; Ray Dolatta, Terry, MT; Wayne Hienbaught, Glendive, MT; and Erv and Marilyn Haidle, Fallon, MT. Fran and Bill Fleckenstein, Terry, MT.

A Special Thanks to Jody Battaglia, my editor.

Certainly, tremendous thanks go to those historical authors for their many fine books about these Indian War Campaigns. Their individual efforts are very much appreciated by us that are students of the American Indian Wars.

Chapter 1

Pompey's Pillar

Pompey's Pillar Sign, the pillar is behind the sign on the left side.

R. KENT MORGAN

Pompey's Pillar

Other Names: Pompey's Tower
Location: From Billings, going northeast on I-94, drive 31 miles until you see the monument road signs to Pompey's Pillar. These are well noted on the map. You can see the Sandstone Pillar from the interstate.

Campaign Name: Lewis and Clark Corps of Discovery 1804 – 1806
Date: July 25, 1806
Principal Commander: Captain William Clark, Co-Commander of Expedition
Forces Engaged: None
Casualties: None

On July 25, 1806 Captain William Clark stopped at this site on his way down the Yellowstone River. In his journal he noted that the rock he named Pompey's Tower stood 200 feet high, was 400 paces in circumference, and only accessible from one side. That nature had engraved animal figures into the rock close to where he carved his name, date and year. This is the only physical evidence left along the journey of the Lewis and Clark's Corps of Discovery.

At the Pillar there is a small gift shop that provides a history of the area. You can also purchase a *National Park Passport* valid at all national parks. This will give you admission to the Little Bighorn Battlefield. The Rosebud battle site is a State Park. Outside the gift shop, stairs will lead you to the spot where William Clark carved his name into the sandstone. Park rangers on duty can provide an excellent history of the pillar, the animals carved by nature, and of Clark's expedition down the Yellowstone. Approximately 25 yards from the base of the pillar, is a reproduction of the type of wooden dugout boat that would have been used. You can also walk to the edge of the Yellowstone River and picnic. This particular area would have been a point for buffalo to migrate across the river.

Clark's party camped a few miles down the Yellowstone that night, and noted that the buffalo made so much noise, it was difficult to sleep.

William Clark's signature

Chapter 2

Fort Pease

Other Names: None

Location: On I-94 drive to Custer. Take the first exit. At the stop sign, turn left turn under the interstate, and cross over the Yellowstone River. Take the first right turn at the Fort Pease Bottom Road. Drive 10.3 miles to Cunningham's Ranch.

GPS Position: 46o 08.718N X 107o 32.870W Elev. 2703' at entrance

Drive to ranch house to obtain permission to see the Fort Pease Bronze Plaque in the front of the house.

GPS Position: 46o 13.779N X 107o 25.737W Elev. 2614' at plaque

Campaign Name: Yellowstone Expedition (1876)

Date: May to September, 1876

Principal Commanders: Brigadier General Alfred Howe Terry and Colonel John Gibbons

Forces Engaged: 20,000 Troops under Terry

Fort Pease basically was a supply depot during the Yellowstone Expedition.

It was founded in late 1875 by a group of traders from Bozeman, Montana, and lead by Major Fellows D. Pease, Zedok H. Daniels and Paulinas W. McCormick.

They constructed a trading post on the north bank of the Yellowstone a few miles from its confluence with the Big Horn River. It was never intended to be a military post. Rather, the traders believed that as a settlement developed, steamboat traffic would increase on the Yellowstone providing them an opportunity to exploit their location. [1]

Hostile Indians put the trading post under constant siege until February, 1876. The post then requested aid from the military, which arrived in March, 1876. They found six men killed, eight wounded and nineteen survivors. All returned to Fort Ellis with Major James Brisbin. The post remained abandoned until June, 1876. Because the Yellowstone River has changed course over the last 128 years, Fort Pease sits on what is now an island in a swampy area about 100 yards directly across from the Cunningham's Ranch house. The road directly in front of this house is the actual military road traveled. It was at this location that Terry and Gibbons dropped off supplies in 1876 for the Yellowstone Expedition against the hostile Sioux Indians.

Note: While Paul McCormick and James Edwards were out hunting on July 12, 1875, a Sioux war party attacked them. McCormick made it back safely to the post, but Edwards had fallen off his horse after being shot several times, and was then seen being scalped by the Sioux. This event occurred near a creek which later became known as Edwards Creek.[2]

GPS Position: 46o 13.569N X 107o 26.625W Elev. 2725' approximately 1/5 miles from entrance to Cunningham's Ranch heading back to Custer is Edward's Creek.

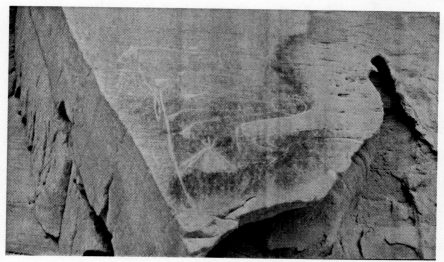

Note: At 2.5 miles heading toward the Cunningham Ranch on the Fort Pease Road. On the left hand side, perhaps 30 feet from the road, are rock cliffs, at the base of which is a pictograph from 3 to 6 feet high. It shows seven rifles lined up horizontally, pointed at a half horse and shield. At eleven to one o'clock there are four arrows pointing towards the shield and the horse at three to four o'clock. At about seven o'clock, just to the right of a lance with feathers and scalps, is a teepee. The rifles are lined up from eight to ten o'clock pointed towards the shield and horse. Just under the rifles pointing vertically from seven to eleven o'clock, is a lance with one feather at ten o'clock, and two scalps at eight o'clock.

GPS Position: 46o 09.572N X 107o 30.309W Elev. 2732' It is 7.8 miles further to Cunningham's Ranch.

---

1.   Website: **www.du.edu/~dhagen/pease.html** Relief of Fort Pease
2.   Extract from Term paper written by Tiffany Cunningham Ogren

Chapter 3

Fort Keogh

One of the Officer's Quarters from Ft. Keogh

R. KENT MORGAN

Fort Keogh

Other Names: Tongue River Post
Location: The fort is well marked at the western edge of Miles City, MT on I-94 exit # 135 headed east. The first left turn takes you to Fort Keogh Livestock and Range Research Laboratory.

GPS Position: 46o 22. 902N X 105o 53. 024W, Elev. 2384' at Research Office Flag Pole

Campaign: Nez Perce Campaign and Bannock Indian Skirmish
Date: September 30 to October 5, 1877 at Bear Paw Mountains and August, 1878 Clark's Fork respectively
Principal Commander: Colonel Nelson A. Miles and Brigadier General O.O. Howard

Forces Engaged: 200 to 300 Troops (Nez Perce Campaign)
Approximately 800 Nez Perce Indians
40 Troops and 75 Crow Scouts against 100 Bannock Indians

Casualties: 20% of Troops and 30% of Indians killed or wounded at Bear Paw Mountain (Nez Perce Campaign), One scout and one officer killed, two troops wounded at Clark's Fork, fourteen Bannock Indians killed, and 30 captured at Clark's Fork

Fort Keogh has been replaced by the Livestock and Range Research Laboratory. Only one original building still stands at the original fort site-a two-story structure with a white stone foundation located next to the Research Office. To drive around the Fort Keogh area, you must first stop at the Research Office, near the flagpole, to obtain the combination to the locks on the gates and an area map. There are still two Officer's quarters that have been moved to the roadside entering old Miles City. After leaving the Fort Keogh driveway, turn left to the Range Rider Museum. The two officer's quarters are off to your left hand side.

Fort Keogh, named after Captain Myles W. Keogh (who died at Little Bighorn), was established and built in 1877 by Colonel Nelson A. Miles' Fifth Infantry. It was huge for its day, with no stockade built around it. A diorama can be seen at the Range Rider Museum. It was at this location on July 16 and 17, 1877, that Lieutenant General William T. Sherman visited and personally presented 31 Medals of Honor to the troops on parade.

In 1876, Colonel Miles' command was stationed two miles east of Fort Keogh, where the Range Rider Museum now stands. The fort actually was authorized for construction in 1876, but the water level of the Yellowstone River was too low for the steamboats carrying the necessary building supplies to reach them. They were forced to wait a year until after the winter thaw created higher water levels.

It was from Fort Keogh, on September 18, 1877, that Colonel Miles led the mounted Fifth Infantry to the Bear Paw Mountains, located in northwest Montana, just south of Chinook on Route 240. Here they intercepted the Nez Perce, who were retreating to Canada. The government was concerned that the Nez Perce would ally themselves with Sitting Bull's Sioux, then in Canada. Chief Joseph surrendered his tribe to Colonel Nelson Miles and General Oliver Howard. The Nez Perce were taken back to Fort Keogh to be transported to Fort Leavenworth, then ultimately to Eastern Washington at the Colville Reservation. Chief Joseph eventually died there, some believe of a broken heart. He also was buried at Colville, but it has been rumored that his remains were secretly re-interred in the Wallowa Valley of northeastern Oregon, the original home of the Nez Perce. Nine Medals of Honor, recommended by Colonel Miles, were awarded from this battle.

The Bannock Indian skirmish started out as a pleasure trip for Miles and some civilians to see the Yellowstone parklands. Just as the expedition neared the mountains, information arrived that a band of one hundred hostile Bannock warriors and their families had left their reservation in Idaho, and were crossing the parklands using same trail as the Nez Perce did in 1877. Miles commissioned Lieutenant

Baldwin to escort the civilians to Fort Ellis, near Bozeman. He then sent Lieutenant Bailey to Boulder Pass with forty troops. He himself led thirty five troops to Clark's Pass. Assistance was enlisted from Crow Warriors from the nearby reservation. Seventy five Crow answered the request. On September 4, 1878, Miles shot his way into the Bannock camp killing fourteen Indians, and capturing thirty more. Miles' force suffered two wounded and one scout killed. Captain Andrew Bennett was killed with a shot through the heart. Although Miles recalled the civilians to continue their pleasure trip, grief over the death of Captain Bennett shortened the trip to some three days, and they returned to Fort Keogh.

Additional information:

On July 16 and 17, 1877, Lieutenant General William T. Sherman visited with Department Commander Brigadier General Alfred H. Terry and Department of Dakota Quartermaster Major Benjamin C. Card. General Sherman personally presented Medals of Honor to the enlisted men who were involved in the 1876 and 1877 winter campaigns: twenty nine for the battle at Cedar Creek, October 21, 1876, two for Wolf Mountain, January 8, 1877. [1] Colonel Miles was considered both within the Military and by the Government to be their best Indian fighting commander, because he and his men had achieved such outstanding results.

During the July 1877 visit to Fort Keogh, Lieutenant General William T. Sherman sent a premature message to the Secretary of War indicating that the Indian Wars were over. [3]

Note: The twenty nine medals presented for Cedar Creek accounted for the most ever awarded for any one Indian battle. The recipients are named below under Cedar Creek Battle. [2]

Medals of gallantry were eventually awarded to three officers for their actions at Battle of Wolf Mountains, January 8,1876, sometimes called Twin Buttes Battle or Tongue River Battle.

Five more medals were awarded for gallantry for Lame Deer. The recipients are named under the Lame Deer Fight, May 7, 1877.

For a complete explanation of Medals of Honor, please refer to Appendix #1.

Fort Keogh garrison was ordered to leave for the Philippines in May 1907, per War Department General Order 112. The fort was closed on October 27, 1908 pursuant to Special Order 146 of the Department of Dakota.

Chapter 4

Tongue River Cantonment

Other Names: First known as Cantonment on Tongue River, or new post on the Yellowstone River or Tongue River Barracks
Location: Western edge of Miles City, Montana, I-94, Exit #135, (named after the Tongue River confluence into the Yellowstone) is two miles from Fort Keogh going east into old Miles City on the left side. It sits at the current site of the Range Rider Museum.

Campaign: Winter Campaign 1876 and 1877
Date: September 1876 to June 1877
Principal Commander: Colonel Nelson A. Miles
Forces Engaged: Fifth Infantry
Casualties: None

The Range Rider Museum is an excellent museum and a must see for the Indian Campaigns and area's history. The museum is extensive and contains dioramas of both Fort Keogh and Lame Deer Battle.

The original cantonment was established and built in 1876 by Colonel Miles' Fifth Infantry to conduct winter campaigns against the Indians in order to drive them back to the reservations. The Cantonment was very crudely and roughly constructed of cottonwood logs chinked with mud and straw. The floor was dirt. It provided a bare minimum of protection from the direct elements and was by no means comfortable. It was officially manned until November 8, 1877 when Fort Keogh was ready.

It was from the Tongue River Cantonment that Col. Nelson Miles led the famous Fifth Infantry on their highly successful winter campaigns against the Sioux. His orders were to totally subdue the non-agency Indians and have them return to their reservations. Four significant battles were fought from this humble location;

1) Cedar Creek Battle, October 21, 1876, against Sitting Bulls', Hunpapas Sioux.
2) Ash Creek Battle, sometimes referred to as Red Water Battle, December 18, 1876, against Sitting Bulls' Hunpapas Sioux
3) Wolf Mountain Battle, sometimes referred to as Twin Buttes or Tongue River Battle, January 18, 1877, against Crazy Horse's Ogalala Sioux
4) Lame Deer Battle, May 7, 1877, against Lame Deer's, Miniconjou Sioux.

It was the Cedar Creek Battle that collapsed the confederation of Sioux, after which most drifted back to the reservations.

1. Greene, Yellowstone Command, p. 223
2. Ibid, p. 223
3. Ibid, p. 223

Chapter 5

Prairie County Museum – Terry, Montana

Other Names: None
Location: On I-94 headed east, Exit 176 drive straight to Spring first stop sign turn left drive ¼ mile to So. Logan turn right to 101 So. Logan the Museum is in an old Bank Building.

GPS Position: 46o 47.59N X 105o 18.448W, Elev. 2265 at exit

Campaign: None
Date: None
Principal Commander: Town named after Brigadier General Alfred H. Terry
Forces Engaged: None
Casualties: None

The town of Terry did not exist at the time of Yellowstone Expedition, but across the Yellowstone at confluence of the Powder River was a Supply Depot. This area contains two gravesites.

The Prairie County Museum in Terry is excellent. A must see for the area's history, as well as the famous Lady Cameron's photos of the early 20th century: machinery, railroad influence and military items. The museum folks are very pleasant and asked them about the scenic route north of Terry.

This area north of the Yellowstone was once prime country where millions of buffalo migrated north into Canada, along with the Indians that depended so heavily on this resource for food, clothing, shelter and robes for trading.

There are two battlefield sites located 33 miles northeast of Terry, which are the Cedar Creek Battlefield and four miles north of Cedar Creek Battlefield is the Ash Creek Battlefield, (also known as the Redwater Creek Battlefield). [1]

Also located about five miles southwest of Terry, on Route 10, was the location of the Powder River Depot. Driving southwest, just before the bridge over the Powder River, you will find a dirt road along side of the Powder River Bridge. Follow the road around the hill to the Yellowstone. Beside the dirt road is the gravesite of Westley "Yank" Brockmeyer, Scout, who was killed by the Sioux. Travel another ½ mile along same road, and you find the gravesite of Trooper William George, who was mortally wounded at the Little Bighorn (at Reno's defensive position), and died en route to Fort Abraham Lincoln while on board the steamboat Far West, captained by Grant Marsh.

Directly across the Yellowstone is Sheridan's Butte. This is quite a climb, but at least two troopers did so in 1876 and cut their names into the sandstone on the west side of the Butte. I rode up to the top of this Butte with my friend Gary Larsen to locate the names but we couldn't find but I have seen pictures of the rock with the two names inscribed.

Further along route 10 there is a sign on the right side heading south, commemorating the approximate location of a meeting between Father Pierre Jean DeSmet, a mediator sent by the Government to discuss the terms of the *Fort Laramie Treaty of 1868* with Sitting Bull on June 19, 1868. Although the discussions were peaceable, Sitting Bull and his Hunkpapa village had no intention of signing this treaty.

Continue on Route 10 and drive another five minutes south to:

GPS Position 46o 42 . 425N X 105o 28. 779W, Elev. 2230. Take a right turn onto a dirt road, go down to the first curve and see the much-noted Buffalo Rapids across the Yellowstone River.

Trivia: When the water level fell in the late summer, the Yellowstone was impossible to navigate past Buffalo Rapids, where rocks stretch across the Yellowstone. These can be seen mid summer through early fall, or whenever the water level is low. Many books refer to the Buffalo Rapids as a real problem for the steamboats on the Yellowstone, which took supplies to the Tongue River Cantonment. When the water level was sufficiently low, wagon trains of supplies headed overland from the Glendive Cantonment.

---

1. O'Neil, Fighting Men of the Indian Wars, p. 39

Chapter 6

Cedar Creek Battlefield and Sitting Bull's Village

The beginning of the battlefield, looking east

The Indian village, looking NW. .

Cedar Creek Battlefield and Sitting Bull's Village

Other Names: None

Location: From I-94, Exit 176 to Terry, Montana, drive directly north on Route #253 across the Yellowstone Bridge. Proceed fourteen miles and approximately twenty minutes, on black top road to the Cedar Creek Road, a gravel road. Take a right turn and proceed past the Grue's Ranch, the first ranch you come to at:

GPS Position 46o 56. 685N X 105o 29. 410W, Elev. 2685'.

There are three views to see both the village and battlefield as follows:

First view: Continue past Ranch two miles to Brackett Creek Road, turn right and continue one mile to the top of the hill. There, on the left hand side, is a sign on the fence for parking area A-7. You are at:

GPS Position 47o 04 .180N X 105o 31. 279W, Elev. 3233.

Looking North on your compass, at 300o and you will see the wooded creek bottom of the East Fork of the Cedar Creek. That was the location of Sitting Bull's Village during the battle.

Second view: (the best view) of both the Battlefield and the Indian Village, just continue up the hill about 300 yards from Parking Area A-7. From here you can park and climb to the first high knoll:

GPS Position : 47o 04.039N X 105o 31.141W, Elev. approx. 3533'.

On compass heading 280o west, approximately three miles away, is the battlefield. It is a series of wooded ravines and prairie with an escarpment on the northeast side.

The Indian Village can be seen at compass heading 300o northwest, approximately 1 and a half-to two miles running north to south, following the east fork of the Cedar Creek. Just look for the trees that follow the creek. The village was on both sides of the creek. During the time of the battle, there were no trees because the buffalo either ate the shoots or trampled the young trees.

Optional view: For more of a bird's eye view, go to the highest point on the ridge and use the same compass headings for battlefield and village sites.

Third view: Retrace your route to Cedar Creek Road and turn right. Continue driving for approximately one mile, where you will drive over a cattle crossing with a fence line running east/west direction. Approximately 300 yards on the left, you can turn off on to the prairie and stop:

GPS Position: 47o 04. 821N X 105o 32. 955W, Elev. 3237.

Campaign: Winter Campaign 1876 and 1877
Date: October 21 to 25, 1876
Principal Commanders: Colonel Nelson Miles
Chief's Sitting Bull and Gall
Forces Engaged: 461 Troops[1]
500 to 600 Indians[2]
Other estimates up to 1000 Indians engaged

Casualties: Two Troops wounded[3]
Five Indians dead[3]

Note: While driving along Route #253 notice the unique rock formations on the left-hand side. This rock formation is in the shape of a house with a pyramid roof. A friend's father dubbed this "Chocolate Butte".

Standing at the views noted above, for miles around you was the actual battlefield, fought on a cold day of October 21, 1876. Try to visualize: You are surrounded by a very dense, choking smoke from Indians firing the prairie at the beginning of the battle. As if in a shroud, the burning prairie crackles and radiates heat. At times you can't see the trooper five paces from you due to the smoke. Some eight hundred to a thousand warriors on horseback are surrounding you, all yelling and blowing their eagle whistles at a high pitched shrill, then charging forward to fire their rifles. Your NCOs scream orders to "Stay in line, adjust your sights, and mark your targets!", as bullets sing over your head or even closer, like a swarm of mad bees. Your company commander is riding a horse behind you shouting "Steady men, stay in ranks, mark your targets men, mark your targets!" You hear the shriek of the Rodman Canon projectile and hear it explode. Your adrenalin is pumping, yet you continue walking ever forward to press the attack. Under such conditions, it is only grit and raw courage that sees you through.

At Third View looking at your compass heading west 240o approximately one mile, is the location of the beginning of the battle, forward of the escarpment. Directly behind and to the east at 90o approximately a mile, is the Sitting Bull's village site.

After the battle began the Indians were concerned with the evacuation of their women and children (estimated at between 2000 to 3000), and possessions from the village site. While the approximately five- to six hundred warriors successfully delayed the attacking troops with harassing gunfire and firing the prairie, the main tribe retreated over Brackett Creek Hill (now parking area A-7). They headed east across Brackett Creek Valley to the hills in the distance, which were called Bad Route Creek. Once over these, the Indians turned south and headed to the Yellowstone River. During the retreat, Sitting Bull and estimated 240 people (or thirty lodges), broke off and headed north to the Fort Peck area as the rest continued to retreat south to the Yellowstone.

Upon reaching the Yellowstone, they walked another few miles east to Cracker Box Creek and forded the Yellowstone to Cabin Creek on the south side. They continued another two miles inland and set up a temporary camp.

Colonel Miles' troops followed the Indians some 40 miles in four days, then halted where Bad Route Creek empties into the Yellowstone. Miles' scouts confirmed the location of the village on Cabin Creek. The author actually discovered the existence of a warrior's gravesite just northeast of the Cabin Creek campsite; I believe that this warrior died from wounds received either during the Cedar Creek battle or the retreat.

During the next couple of days, the Indians parleyed with Colonel Miles and surrendered. Some five Chiefs were kept as hostages, as the remaining Indians agreed to hunt while proceeding south to the Red Cloud Agency. These five chiefs were sent to Glendive Cantonment, then on to Fort Buford to catch steamboats to the Indian agency. Miles was concerned that Sitting Bull had eluded capture, so he wanted to reorganize and pursue him aggressively.

Miles troops then march back to Tongue River Cantonment for re-supply, and headed north to Fort Peck to intercept Sitting Bull.

Note: The beginning of the Cedar Creek Battle was located at **GPS Position: 47o 04. 624N, X 105o 33. 696W, Elev. 3215**, compass heading 340o northeast, approximately one mile off the Cedar Creek Road. This site now lays on private property, and permission is needed for access.

The actual Indian Village Site, also now on private property, requires permission for access and is located at:

GPS Position: 04. 920N, X 105o 32. 153W, Elev. 3132.

Author's notes taken from walking over each site:

The beginning of the battle site is situated in a small valley perhaps one thousand yards across. There is a rocky ridge, or escarpment, perhaps 300 feet high on the northeast side, with narrow, wooded ravines in the center. On the southeast side, Becker Dam can be seen from the ridge, one quarter-to one-half mile trailing to the south.

The battle proceeded to the east over the Cedar Creek Road (where you can park your car) and down the slopes into the village site. The land is prairie with several ravines and gulches consisting of a mix of sandstone, shale, dirt and gravel, with several areas of dense ground covering of creeping cedar, grass and sage. At several random spots I stopped and scratched the surface of the prairie floor; about one to one half inches down I found burnt earth, which indicates or perhaps confirms, that the prairie in this location had at one time suffered a fire. Walking over the battlefield I found no artifacts, on the ridge or escarpment that was cleared of Indians during the beginning of the battle. The ridge is gravel, sandstone and rock shale that is loose. Several mudflows are evident along both sides of the ridge.

The troops marched in skirmish formation (five paces apart), to approximately where you are standing at the third view crossed over the Cedar Creek Road and continued east to the village site, then southeast following the retreating Indians, site of the first view.

Two troopers were wounded and five Indians were killed during this opening battle. After dark, the troops camped near the foot of the ridge that was captured at the beginning of the battle. The troops had marched and fought approximately 18 miles that day. During the night, the Indians harassed the troops with distant rifle fire, making sleep fitful for the troops.

The Indian's village camp was along the creek bottom and situated on gentle slopes. I found no teepee stone rings in this area, because there are no large stones in or near the creek bottom. I did find evidence of teepee rings along the west side of the creek. The Indians would have removed the dirt from the higher side of the slope and spread it out to form a flat, level foundation, then erected their teepees on this surface. I discovered at least 20 to 30 rings averaging approximately 18 feet in diameter.

I walked from the beginning of battlefield to the Indian village site and discovered no artifacts. I talked to the ranch owner, who indicated that this was a sheep grazing area for several years, and herders may have collected any artifacts that may have been on the surface. The Terry Museum has several shell casings and bullets from around this area.

Note: A local rancher indicated that when the land first was ranched the in late 1880s, there were no trees, even around the creek bottoms. I can only guess that buffalo herds moving through this area would have either eaten or trampled any new sprouts. Even now, after 126 years, the trees, mostly cottonwood, are no more than twenty feet high.

The Cantonment Post Returns dated October 31, 1876 contains the following entries:

"22nd Infantry Co. E & F join cantonment on October 2, 1876.

Colonel Miles' 5th Infantry with regiment left October 17th on an expedition against hostile Indians who had made attack on the supply train en-route from Glendive Creek.

They marched 12 miles to a point on Cedar Creek where, on the October 21st they engaged the Indians, (number estimated at 500 to 600) under Sitting Bull. Sergeant Robert. McPhalin, Co. "E" and Pvt. John Geyer, Co. "I" 5th Infantry wounded in action. Pursuing the Indians up Cedar Creek. Across to Bad Route Creek and down the same to the Yellowstone, 64 miles where on the 24th Red Shirt, Bull Eagle, and other chiefs representing some 400 lodges of Minniconjoes and Cheyenne surrendered. Sitting Bull with about 30 lodges retreated North.

Col. Miles with a portion of the command returned to cantonment early on the morning of the 31st to refit for a scout towards Dry Fork of the Missouri distance marching in returning 90 miles. "

Miles had written his wife Mary a letter telling her that he was very pleased with his troops in battle. Everyone was engaged, and field maneuvers were carried out effectively and efficiently with precision. He was extremely proud of his troops' successes.[4]

Fifth Infantry Command and Medals of Honor awarded:

Commanding Officer Colonel (Brevet Major General) Nelson Appleton Miles

Miles' Adjutant First Lieutenant George W. Baird

Company Commanders:

Company A: Captain James S. Casey
Company B: Captain Andrew S. Bennett
Company C: Captain Edmond Butler
Company D: First Lieutenant Robert McDonald
Company E: Second Lieutenant James Worden Pope
Company F: Captain Simon Snyder, in support of cannon
Company G: First Lieutenant Theodore F. Forbes
Company H: Second Lieutenant David Q. Rousseau
Company I: Captain Wyllys Lyman
Company J: Not in action
Company K: First Lieutenant Mason Carter
Wagons: Second Lieutenant William H.C. Bowen
Pack animals: Second Lieutenant James H. Whitten [6]

Company disposition during the battle:

Miles' troops approach the village from the west, attacking east and driving the Indians to southeast. Company commanders and Medal of Honor recipients by company:

Company A: Captain James S. Casey, north end of line sweeping thenorthern flank of the escarpment.

Medal of Honor recipients:
David Holland, Cpl., Born: Dearborn, MI
Fred O. Hunt, Pvt., Born: New Orleans, LA
John McHugh, Pvt., Born: Syracuse, NY
Michael McLoughlin, Sgt., Born: Ireland
David Roche, First Sgt., Born: Ireland
Henry Rodenburg, Pvt., Born: Germany
Charles Sheppard, Pvt ., Born: Rocky Hill, CN

Company B: Captain Andrew S. Bennett, next to Company A, north end of line.

Medal of Honor recipient:
John Haddoo, Corporal, Born: Boston, Massachusetts

Company C: Captain Edmond Butler, next to Company B, center of the line.

Medal of Honor recipients:
James S. Calvert, Pvt., Born: Athens County, OH
Edward Johnston, Cpl., Born: Pen Yan, NY
Aquilla Coonrod, Sgt., Born: Williams County, OH
Philip Kennedy, Pvt., Born: Ireland
Wendelin Kreher, First Sgt., Born: Prussia
Owen McGar, Pvt., Born: North Attleboro, MA
William Wallace, Sgt., Born: Ireland
Patton G. Whitehead, Pvt., Born: Russell County, VA

Company I: Capt. Wyllys Lyman next to Company C, south end of line.

Medal of Honor recipients:
Joseph A. Cable, Pvt., Born: Cape Girardeau, MO
Charles H. Montrose, Pvt., Born: St. Louis, MO

Company K: First LT. Mason Carter, next to Company I, extreme south end of line.

No recommendations for Medal of Honor

Company H, Second Lt. David Q. Rousseau, assisted Capt. Casey in routing the Indians on the northern most flank along, and on top of, the escarpment.

Medal of Honor recipients;
George Miller, Cpl., Born: Brooklyn, NY
Charles Wilson, Cpl., Born: Petersburg, Il
— Inducted: Beardstown, IL (author's hometown)

Company E: Second Lt. James W. Pope routed the Indians on the southern-most flank.

Medal of Honor recipient;
Robert McPhelan, Sgt., Born: Ireland; one of two troopers wounded at the village site.
Company F: Capt. Simon Snyder supported the Rodman Gun while positioned on a knoll southwest of the front lines. Second Lt. Pope assisted in keeping Indians from flanking the Rodman Gun.

No Recommendations for Medal of Honor

Company G: First Lt. Theodore F. Forbes, was in reserve.

Medal of Honor recipients:
    Richard Burke, Pvt., Born: Ireland
    Denis Byrne, Sgt., Born: Ireland
    John S. Donelly, Pvt., Born: Buffalo, NY
    Henry Hogan, First Sgt., Born: Ireland **
    Michael McCormick, Pvt., Born: Rutland, VT
    David Ryan, Pvt., Born: Ireland

Company D: First Lt. Robert McDonald guarded the wagon train.

Medal of Honor recipients:
    Christopher Freemeyer, Pvt., Born: Germany
    Edward Rooney, Pvt., Born: Poughkeepsie, NY

Two other men received medals for "Acts of Gallantry" at Cedar Creek. They were:

John Baker, Musician Company D
Bernard McCann, Pvt. Company F, 22nd Infantry (Awarded Posthumously)

These medals were actually awarded on April 27, 1877 by General T. Sherman, Lieutenant General, and Chief of Army at Fort Keogh, Montana

Most of the Citations simply read: "Gallantry in action" [6]

First Sergeant Wendelin Kreher, Sergeant, Aquilla Coonrod, Corporal John Haddoo, and Private Bernard McCann are actually buried at Custer's National Cemetery.

** Henry Hogan, First Sergeant, was awarded a Medal of Honor for Cedar Creek battle and a second medal for Nez Perce Battle of Bear Paw Mountains on September 30, 1877, only double recipient for the Indian Wars. Note: First Lt. Frank D. Baldwin received a second Medal of Honor for his participation in the Red River Indian Campaign.

These 31 Medals of Honor were the most awarded for any battle, making up seven per cent of the 423 Medals awarded during the Indian Wars.

Note: First Lieutenant Frank D. Baldwin, who was awarded two medals, one from the Civil War, and one from the Indian Wars (Red Water Expedition), was on detached duty to Fort Leavenworth during the Battle of Cedar Creek.

Companies A, B, C, I, and K made up the front line to attack the village.
Troops fought for some eight miles on October 21, 1876. [6]

The author is particularly interested in this site because;

1.   Most Medal of Honors every awarded for an Indian war battle.
2.   First face to face meeting and battle between Sitting Bull and an Army commander.
3.   No sign or monument denotes this battlefield.

---

1. Greene, Yellowstone Command, p. 90
2. Ibid, p. 102
3. Ibid p. 104
4. Ibid, p.104
5. Ibid, p. 94.
6. Ibid, p. 102, Johnston, A cold Day in Hell, p.vii – xiv, O'Neil, Fighting Men of the Indian Wars, p.31, **www.army.mil/cmh-pg/mohind.htm** Information about the Medal of Honor during Indian War Period.

Chapter 7

Ash Creek Battlefield

Ash Creek Battlefield looking NW toward the village site.

R. KENT MORGAN

Ash Creek Battlefield

Other Names: Red Water Battlefield
Location: After viewing Cedar Creek Battlefield drive approximately five miles north on Cedar Creek Road, keeping to the left.

At GPS Position 47o 07.682N X 105o 38. 198W, Elev. 3179 you will see a gate on your left hand side. If you park at the gate there is a dirt road that slopes down to a barn ¼ mile. Looking northwest 340o, you can see a Pyramid Monument on top of a high knoll to the left of the barn. The trees to the right following the creek bottom are where the Indian village stood about ¼ mile.

Campaign: Winter Campaign 1876 and 1877
Date: December 18, 1876
Principal Commanders: Lieutenant Frank Dwight Baldwin
Chief Sitting Bull
Forces Engaged: 110 Troops[1]
600 Indians[2]
Casualties: None

On November 5,1876, after the Cedar Creek Battle, Colonel Miles, along with Lieutenant Baldwin, marched up to Fort Peck on the Missouri River looking for Sitting Bull and his band that had escaped during the retreat at Cedar Creek.

Miles split his command on December 1, 1876 and ordered Baldwin to take three companies of men and thirty wagons to Fort Peck, then to Wolf Point and onto Fort Buford in hope that Baldwin would perhaps come across some hostiles and drive them back to the reservation. Miles would take the command north and then drive south.

Before departing Miles said, "Baldwin, you know my plans and what is desired to be accomplished. I know you will do the best you can. I shall be anxious until I hear from you. If you meet with ill success, I can take the responsibility for the movement; if you are successful, it will be very creditable to you. I hope you will be successful. If you do no more than keep them moving, you will do well." [3]

On December 7, 1876, Baldwin and his troops fought a brief skirmish with Sitting Bull and his followers at Big Muddy near Milk River, then retreated back to Fort Peck.

On December 10, 1876, word arrived that Sitting Bull had moved to a location into the valley of the Redwater River. Baldwin ordered his troops to mobilize and march southeast to the Redwater River, hoping to engage Sitting Bull's village.

After marching and enduring deep snow, rough terrain, wind and bitter cold (40 degrees below zero), on December 13th and 14th, Baldwin rested his troops. Many had become sick and suffered frostbite due to the harsh elements. Baldwin continued on with his march southwestwardly. On December 18, 1876 at about 1:00 PM, after passing through badlands, Baldwin came to a hollow that beheld Sitting Bull's village. There were 120 lodges and on nearby prairies some 350 head of horses. [4]

The confrontation was a short one, the troops attacked in skirmish order as Baldwin ordered a cannon fired upon the village. The troops drove the Indians out of camp so quickly the Indians left behind sixty head of livestock, hundreds of buffalo robes, large quantities of meat, sugar, tea, flour, calico red cloth and blankets that denied these essentials to the Indians during this harsh winter. Baldwin's men, starving, cold and sick, stopped long enough to eat captured meat and then burned what they couldn't carry away. [4]

The troops followed the retreating Indians for some six miles with no further contact, then marched on to the Tongue River Cantonment. The ease of driving the Indians from the village was due to the fact that most of the warriors were out hunting before the attack began. There were no causalities on either side. [4]

Baldwin sent a message on to the cantonment to notify Colonel Miles of his engagement and its favorable results, which delighted Miles.

Note: The author has walked the village site and its terrain. It is rolling prairie with steep escarpments. The village site was pretty well hidden below the hills, tucked into the creek bottom, thus protecting it from the hash winds. There is a natural spring very close to the village site that would have provided fresh running water year round. About three miles south of the village site, the creek turns to the east. The retreat would have taken the Indians to the divide, then east over the same ground as the Cedar Creek battlefield retreat route.

Top left picture is the site of the monument today. The top right picture is village site by the trees, bottom left picture is aerial view of monument hill and bottom right picture is the plaque

1.   Steinbach, A Long March, p.220
2.   Ibid, p.111
3.   Ibid, p.110
4.   Ibid, p.114 & 115

Chapter 8

Glendive Cantonment

Other Names: Glendive Depot
Location: From Terry, drive east on I-94 to US Route #16 heading to Sidney. Traveling north approximately three miles, you will pass a Grain Elevator on your right. Take the very next right onto a dirt road. Follow this dirt road to the railroad tracks and stop. On the right side was the site of the Glendive Cantonment. It actually was from the edge of the river up to and across the railroad track to the slight embankment. This area is private property.

GPS Position: 47o 09.085N X 104o 41.755W, Elev. 2065
At the Railroad Tracks

Campaign: Supported both Yellowstone Expedition and Winter Campaign
Date: Established at the beginning of the Yellowstone Expedition, 1876
Principal Commander: Colonel Elwell S. Otis
Forces Engaged: None
Casualties: None

Note: As you are driving east on I-94, you will see a exit sign for Bad Route Creek, near Glendive. If you pull off the exit and look to your right, you will see where the Sioux, retreating from the Cedar Creek

Battle, crossed the Yellowstone River. If you look to the left you can see the drainage route from which the Indians retreated.

The Glendive Cantonment was established in the summer of 1876, and manned by the 22nd Infantry Commanded by Colonel Elwell S. Otis, who was under the command of Colonel Nelson Miles at the Tongue River Cantonment. It was Otis' task to support the Tongue River Cantonment with supplies that were loaded onto wagons.

Supplies were shipped from Fort Buford via steamboat when the river was high enough, or by wagon trains when the water level was low. Supplies were then reloaded on wagons for shipment to Tongue River Cantonment to support troops during Miles' Winter Campaigns.

It was from this location that a train of over one hundred wagons were in transit when attacked in early October 1876 on the Glendive/Tongue River Wagon Road. These running skirmishes are known as the Spring Creek Battles or Skirmishes. Miles received word that that Colonel Otis' wagon train was under continuous attack by Sitting Bull. Indian spies for Miles also confirmed this.

On October 17, 1876, Miles mobilized the 5th Infantry: some fifteen officers, 434 men, plus ten civilians and four scouts equaling 463 men, who carried fourteen days worth of rations. He crossed the Yellowstone following the wagon road, and marched thirty miles that day, halting at 1:00 AM. [1]

October 18, Troops marched another 14 miles, approximately five miles from the mouth of Custer Creek, meeting Colonel Otis' wagon train. Miles decided to move northeast to intercept the Indians that attacked Otis. [1] Colonel Otis continued to the Tongue River Cantonment with supplies. From this point, on October 21 though the 24 1876, Colonel Miles marched north to engage Sitting Bull and his band at the Cedar Creek Battlefield.

---

1.   Johnston, A Cold Day in Hell, p. 74, 83-91

Chapter 9

Fort Buford and Fort Union

Fort Buford Parade Grounds

R. KENT MORGAN

Fort Buford and Fort Union

Other Names: None
Location: Take US Route 16 to Sidney. From Sidney take Highway 200 to Fairview, then take Highway 58 north to Fort Buford. On Route 1804, one mile away is Fort Union. It is well noted on the map and road signs.

Fort Union, originally a fur trading post, was abandoned and dismantled in 1867.

Campaign: Yellowstone Expedition 1876 and Winter Campaign 1876 and 1877
Date: Established on June 13, 1866
Principal Commander: Colonel William B. Hazen
Forces Engaged: None
Casualties: One Officer, Major George E. Lord, the fort surgeon, died at Little Bighorn with Custer.

 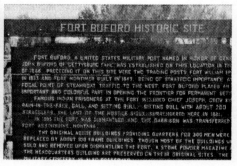

Fort Buford eventually housed six companies of infantry and cavalry. During the early years, it saw very few skirmishes with the Indians. The most troops to serve at this post were 282 men, who were responsible for policing the border with Canada, guarding railroad crews, and escorting steamers and wagon trains, especially down to Glendive Cantonment. During the Indian Campaigns in the south, they were actively involved with moving supplies to the troops. It was at Fort Buford that Sitting Bull surrendered on July

19, 1881, to Major David Brotherton, senior post officer. Sitting Bull was later remanded to Fort Randall where he was arrested. Today, Brotherton's quarters is the site of the museum and the museum store. Very few buildings remain.

In July, the Sixth Infantry Reenactment Group holds an encampment at Fort Buford. A few miles away, the Fort Union Trading Post interprets the fur trade. Fort Buford was abandoned in October 1895.

Fort Union established and built in1828 by John Jacob Astor's American Fur Company. It became a headquarters for trading beaver and buffalo hides with the Assiniboin Indians to the north, the Crow Indians on the upper Yellowstone, and the Blackfeet who lived farther up the Missouri.

This fort has been reconstructed, and is very attractive to see and visit. there are several interpretive shops to see when visiting. The Fort was abandoned in October 1895.

Chapter 10

Powder River Battlefield

Powder River Battlefield - Today

Powder River Battlefield

Other Names: Powder River Fight or Reynolds Battlefield

Location: From Miles City take Highway 59 south to Broadus. Just on the outskirts of Broadus on Highway 212, take the Moorehead Road (route 391) south for 35 miles on gravel road to the Battlefield. A memorial is on the left-hand side. A gate leads you out onto a small plateau, an excellent view for taking pictures above the battlefield. Compass heading 40o east is the actual village site, and bit north and at 140o due south of the monument, at the base of the butte sticking out (the river turns west here) is what is known as Hospital Point. The Battlefield is on private land, but the ranch owners are near Hospital Point and can be contacted for permission.

GPS Position: 45o 06 . 134N X 105o 51. 578W, Elev. 3424

Campaign: Powder River Expedition

Date: March 17, 1876

Principal Commanders: Colonel Joseph J. Reynolds attached to
      Brigadier General George Crook's Command

      Mixed Sioux and Northern Cheyenne Village

Forces Engaged: 389 Troops, including scouts
                  100 lodges estimated at 300 to 400 warriors

Casualties: Four Troops killed and six wounded
              Undetermined number of Indians killed or wounded

The high cliffs on the other side of the road from the monument are where the troops waited in freezing weather to attack the village at dawn. The initial charge on the village was through a large ravine just south of the monument approximately ¼ of a mile through a creek bottom that led from the plateau to the river bottom.

During the battle, the Indians drove north along the river to the plateau where you are standing and to the higher cliffs across the road from the monument, and fired upon the soldiers in the village. They kept up this harassing fire for the duration of time the soldiers were in the village area. Several soldiers were wounded. The Indians successfully recaptured a large number of their horses that night, which the troops had taken during the early morning hours of the attack. Colonel Reynolds' leadership was extremely poor in carrying out General Crook's orders to capture as much food and provisions as possible. Reynolds was later accused of leaving dead and wounded men on the battlefield. General Crook preferred charges and Colonel Reynolds was court marshaled, ending his career.

Crook recommended two men for Medals of Honor as follows:
Albert Glavinski, Blacksmith
Jeremiah Murphy, Private

This is nice drive that parallels the Powder River almost the entire way. On the right side driving south, notice the very unique and beautiful rock formations. My favorite is at **GPS Position 45o 18.121N X 105o 36. 565W, Elev. 3500**.

Note: After backtracking to Highway 212 going west towards Lame Deer, if time allows, you should see the Northern Cheyenne Indian Museum in Ashland, Montana at St. Labre Indian School. It is small but excellent.

Chapter 11

Lame Deer Battlefield and Area

Lame Deer Battlefield site today

R. KENT MORGAN

Lame Deer Battlefield and Area

Other Names: Lame Deer Fight, Muddy Creek Battle, Little Muddy Creek

Location: Lame Deer, Montana on State Route 39 and U.S. 212. Driving west on U.S. 212, take a left on Route 39, or Cheyenne Avenue. Proceed slowly to Ridge Walker St., then go slowly two more blocks south (the streets are not named), make a right turn, go one block west, and make a left turn, go one block. There is a Yellow House with flagpole in the front yard. To the left of which would have been the center of the village attacked.

GPS Position @ 45o 35.587N X 106o 39.751W, Elev. 3308 at the Yellow House with flagpole.

Campaign: Winter Campaign 1876 and 1877
Date: May 7, 1877
Principal Commanders: Colonel Nelson Miles
                              Chief Lame Deer, Miniconjou Sioux
Forces Engaged: 471 Troops [1]
                   Approx. 300 Indians [2]
Casualties: Four Troops killed and ten Wounded[2]
               Approx. 14 Indians killed, including Chief Lame Deer[2]

Lame Deer's First Grave Site
Continue from the yellow house, make a right turn, then a left, to the first group of residential housing. Take a right turn up to the top of the hill. There is a dirt road with deep ruts to follow; look to your right to see the Sand Stone Cliff Caves. In the first large cave on the right was Lame Deer's first gravesite.
Look at compass heading south 200o,
GPS Position 45o 36.258N X 106o 40.274W, Elev. 3484 on road across from gravesite.

Upon returning to Ridge Walker Street and Cheyenne Avenue at:

GPS Position 45o 36.700 N X 106o 39.581W, Elev. 3386 is the approximate location of the Lame Deer's Pony Herd as Colonel Miles attacked the village.

This battle was fought as one of the last remnants of the Indian coalition who had participated in the Battle of the Little Big Horn.

Colonel Miles' command surprised and surrounded Chief Lame Deer's Village in the early morning of May 7, 1877. Miles parleyed with Chief Lame Deer to persuade him to surrender, but a scuffle ensued nearby, and Miles was fired upon, very nearly taking his life. Unfortunately, the trooper next to him was killed.

Note: Chief Crazy Horse and approximately 900 Ogallala Sioux surrendered on May 6, 1877 at the Red Cloud Agency just a day before this battle took place at Lame Deer.

After the Lame Deer Battle, only Chief Sitting Bull and small band of Humkpapa Sioux were at large in Canada. On July 19, 1881, even they would surrender at Fort Buford, ending the Great Sioux War.

Miles recommended five enlisted men to receive the Medal of Honor[3] Corporal Harry Garland , Private William Leonard, Farrier William H. Jones, First Sergeant Henry Wilkens, all from Company "L", 2nd Cavalry, and Private Samuel D. Phillips from Company "H", 2nd Cavalry

Note: Another important site in Lame Deer is the Indian Cemetery where Chief Dull Knife and Chief Little Wolf, both famous Northern Cheyenne War Chiefs are buried side by side.

Location: From the intersection of U.S. Highway 212 and Route 39 take a right turn on to Route 39. Go half a block, take another right turn and drive straight back to the cemetery. Stop at the Indian Veteran memorial and walk up the hill to see the burial sites of Chief Dull Knife and Chief Little Wolf, surrounded by a white fence.

GPS Position: 45o 37.551N X 106o 35.711W, Elev. 3332
Lame Deer Cemetery

Note: As you leave the cemetery entrance, look toward the highway about twenty five yards to your left to see the remains of an old Indian sweat lodge. Notice the skeleton of the branches form an upside down bowl. The Indians would throw buffalo hides over the structure and perform religious ritual within by pouring water over hot rocks for steam.

Note: Another important site in Lame Deer is as you enter the cemetery on the left side of the hill. Here are some painted white rocks and boulders coming down from the top of the hill. This is the path that two young Cheyenne Warriors took for a suicide charge on troops. Both were killed in this attack in the late 1890's. The story is that the warriors killed a young white teenager who surprised them while butchering a steer on his parent's ranch. Having committed this murder, the warriors knew they would be arrested and hung, so they agreed to die as warriors and charged on the troops who were there to arrest them.

Note: Another important site is the Deer Medicine Rocks, the site where Chief Sitting Bull (famous Sun Dance) had a vision of the impending defeat of the soldiers, in which soldiers were falling upside down into the Indian camp. It came to be the Battle of the Little Bighorn, or as the Indian's call it, the "Battle of the Greasy Grass", which occurred some two to three weeks after the vision. The location is exactly four miles from the junction of Highway 212 and Route 39 heading north on Route 39 to Forsyth. Just exiting the Cheyenne Indian Reservation is the John "Jack" Bailey Ranch. Mr. Bailey owns the ranch on which lies Deer Medicine Rocks. If you obtain permission to visit, and he is available, Mr. Bailey will escort you to the rocks and explain the pictographs on them. To the Indians this is sacred ground and should be respected.

Continue north on Route 39 approximately 1.9 miles past the Bailey Ranch and to the left, you can see the Deer Medicine Rocks, which are four very large, vertical rocks about half a mile from the highway. The area to your right is the actual site of Sitting Bull's Sun Dance and vision noted above.

GPS Position: 45o 41.645N X 106o 40.856W, Elev. 3190 to view Deer Medicine Rocks from Highway 39

Note: Continue north on Route 39 approximately another mile or two at **GPS Position 45o 45.450N X 106o 35.992W, Elev. 3045** to view the road side historical marker on the left hand side of highway which indicates where Custer made camp on June 23, 1876, on his way to the Little Big Horn.

1. Greene, Yellowstone Command, p 203
2. Ibid, p. 211 & 212, Johnston, Ashes of Heaven, p. 389, Billington, Soldier and Brave, p.193
3. Website: **www.army.mil/cmh-pg/mohind.htm** Information about the Medal of Honor during Indian War Period.

Chapter 12

Battle of Wolf Mountain

Photo taken on the eastern butte looking west toward the Tongue River by the tree line. The right side in the green pasture was the location of Miles' Troops at the beginning of the battle.   Note: The white sign located by the road indicating Battle of Wolf Mountains.

R. KENT MORGAN

Battle of Wolf Mountain

Other Names: Twin Buttes Fight, Battle of the Buttes, Battle Butte or Miles' Battle of the Tongue River. The Northern Cheyenne call it the Battle of Belly Butte.

Note: There are two routes to this site. You can drive from Lame Deer by taking Route #39 to Birney, or take county road #118 from the Rosebud Battlefield to Birney. To save time, my preference is that after seeing Lame Deer sites, drive to Birney on Route #39, then on to the Rosebud Battlefield. Both directions are given below as noted: From Lame Deer and from The Rosebud Battlefield.

From Lame Deer: Take Route #39 south approximately twenty miles. This is a nice black top road that enters a very small village and crosses over the Tongue River. After crossing over the bridge, it turns into a good gravel road for another eight miles to Birney on your right. Once you enter Birney, a very small village, continue 5.4 miles and stop at the Quarter Circle Ranch to obtain permission to walk the Wolf Mountain Battlefield site. The site is another three miles down from the Ranch. Look for a big white sign on the right hand side between the western and eastern buttes,
GPS Position 45o 17.168N X 106o 34.825W, Elev. 3214' Wolf Mountain Battlefield on road between the two buttes.

After viewing the battlefield site continue south on country road #118 for 22 miles. Upon reaching the black top highway #314, take a right hand turn and drive 4.5 miles west to the entrance to the Rosebud Battlefield on your left.
GPS Position: 45o 13.240N X 106o 56.927W, Elev. 4304' at this entrance.

From The Rosebud Battlefield: Drive out to the entrance and while driving east to Decker at 4.5 miles take the county road #118 to Birney on your left,

GPS Position: 45o 10. 353N X 106o 53. 975W, Elev. 3865'

Drive 22 miles from turn off on to county road #118, a good gravel road. This road winds down the valley to the Tongue River and you cross a bridge over the Tongue River.
GPS Position: 45o 16.090N X 106o 37. 459W, Elev. 3872', not too much further then.

GPS Position: 45o 17.168N X 106o 34. 825W, Elev. 3214' Wolf Mountain Battlefield is on the road between the two buttes

Campaign: 1876-77 Winter Campaign
Date: January 8, 1877
Principal Commanders: Colonel Nelson A. Miles
                                    Chief Crazy Horse leading the Sioux
                                    Chief Two Moons leading the Cheyenne
Forces engaged: Troops: 436 Men
                             Indians: estimated 500 to 600 Warriors
Estimated casualties: Two enlisted men killed and eight wounded
                                     An estimated three Indians killed

Colonel Miles was ordered to carry out a Winter Campaign against "hostiles", or non-reservation Indians. Miles' command was stationed at the Tongue River Containment (Miles City, Montana). Miles had not planned to conduct another winter campaign after the defeating Sitting Bull at Cedar Creek Battlefield on October 21, 1876. On December 18, 1876, warriors attacked a government mail contractor within miles of the post and made off with the mail and several government animals, forcing cancellation of mail service. On December 26, 1876, warriors stole 250 head of cattle from the post. Miles notified department headquarters in St. Paul, Minnesota, and on December 28 led a strike force out of the Tongue River Cantonment.

On Jan 8, 1877 the Battle of Wolf Mountains commenced. This engagement was fought under freezing weather conditions and deep snow at the outset, with a blizzard that followed later in the day as the Indians retreated back to their village. Colonel Miles held the field. This battle produced very few casualties on either side, even though a great amount of ammunition was discharged. After this battle, neither Crazy Horse nor Two Moons would ever mount another attack against the troops.

Note: The high cliffs on your right side looking east would have been well manned and well armed by warriors.

At the battle site location there is a huge white sign on the left hand side indicating the battlefield. If you look at your compass heading 340o, you will see the Tongue River lower down the valley; the trees follow the river. This was the location of Miles' troops at the beginning of the battle. The troops would have deployed and slowly marched up hill to where the sign now is, crossed the road and assaulted the butte directly across the road from the Battlefield sign. Hence the name "Twin Buttes Fight" or "Twin Buttes Battle".

The battle ended in the early afternoon, mainly due to a horrendous snow blizzard. The troops followed the retreating Sioux, but were never able to engage them due to the harsh blizzard conditions.

Miles recommended three Officers and two enlisted men for the Medal of Honor:

Captain Edmond Butler, Private Philip Kennedy, Captain James S. Casey, Private Patton G. Whited and First Lieutenant Robert McDonald.[1]

This battlefield is on private property, but just past the battlefield, up the road a couple miles, the owners live on Quarter Circle "U" Ranch. There you can ask permission to access the battlefield.

---

1. Vaughn, With Crook at the Rosebud, p. 219
2. Hedren, Traveler's Guide to the Great Sioux War, p. 53
3. Website: **www.army.mil/cmh-pg/mohind.htm** Information about the Medal of Honor during Indian War Period.

Chapter 13

Rosebud Battlefield

Rosebud Battlefield taken from Headquarters Hill looking southwest

Rosebud Battlefield

Other Names: Battle of the Rosebud, Rosebud Fight. The Cheyenne called this battle; "Where the Girl Saves Her Brother",

Location: On U.S. Highway 212 west, just a mile from Busby, take a left turn to Decker on Highway 314 heading south. Follow 314 for 20 miles to the battlefield sign. The actual battlefield is about 1.5 miles of dirt road off highway 314.

GPS Position: 45o 13. 240N X 106o 56. 927W, Elev. 4304' entrance to Rosebud Battlefield from Highway 314

Campaign: Yellowstone Expedition
Date: June 17, 1876
Principle Commanders: Brigadier General George Crook, Commander of the Department of the Platte (included present-day Iowa, Nebraska, and Wyoming).

Chief Crazy Horse leading the Confederated Sioux, Chief Two Moon leading the Northern Cheyenne

Forces engaged: Troops: 1,300 men including scouts and miners
Indians estimated between 1,300 to 1,500

Estimated Casualties: Nine Troops killed, and 17 wounded.[1]
Thirty-nine Indians killed, and 63 wounded, [2]
Other estimates approx. 100 wounded.

Note: The Indians always made an attempt to retrieve the dead and wounded from the battlefield.

This battle was fought between General George Crook and Cheyenne and Sioux warriors led by Crazy Horse. This battle fought on June 17th, only eight days before the Battle of Little Bighorn.

Note: While driving south on highway 314 down the Rosebud valley from highway 212 (approximately 15 miles) notice how the valley narrows with the wooded terrain as you get closer to the battlefield turnoff. This was particularly alarming to Captain Mills, as he was ordered by General Crook to scout north for the Indian village following the Rosebud Creek bottom that you are paralleling. Captain Mills was very concerned about being ambushed in the narrow valley, but was ordered back by General Crook to support the battle.

General Crook had been ordered to lead his troops north from Fort Fetterman in Douglas, Wyoming to the Rosebud area, while Colonel John Gibbon was ordered to lead troops east from Fort Ellis in Helena Montana. General Alfred Terry was ordered to lead his troops west from Fort Abraham Lincoln in Bismarck, North Dakota. The Seventh Cavalry was attached to General Terry's command based at Fort Abraham Lincoln.

It was the government's strategy to drive the Indians with this pincer movement for a large battle, or to convince them to return to their reservations.

Crook had approximately 1,300 troops and scouts, picking up some miners along the trail north. His command was surprised by the Cheyenne and Sioux at the headwaters of the Rosebud Creek. If it had not been for the brave and courageous Crow and Shoshone scouting the area, Crook might have suffered more casualties.

It was the Crow and Shoshone Scouts that sounded the alarm and met the first attacking Sioux and Cheyenne some 500 yards from the camp. This delaying action was long enough to give the troops much needed time to get organized and ready for action. This was a full-fledged battle, lasting at least eight hours and covering over ten square miles. Some 1,300 to 1,500 Indians attacked Crook's troops, who were having coffee. Crook was playing cards with some of his officers. The troops drove the Indians back into defensive positions in the latter part of the day, holding the field as night fell.

Although Crook considered this a victory because he held the field, many of his officers and military commanders considered it as a defeat. The Indian scouts were so upset with Crook that they went back to their homes soon after this battle.

Crook repositioned his command back to Goose Creek near present day Sheridan, Wyoming to bivouac until he could get more replacement troops and supplies. This withdrawal from the campaign relieved the pressure on the Indians from the south and possibly contributed to the victory over Custer on June 25th. The Indians claimed the Battle at Rosebud to be their victory.

The Cheyenne dubbed this the battle "Where the Girl Saves her Brother". Legend has it that the Cheyenne named the battle for the heroism of one of their warrior's a women who fearlessly risked her own life to rescue her brother whose mount had been shot out from under him.

"On The Rosebud with Crook", written by Burke, is an excellent book covering this battle.

Crook recommended four enlisted men for the Medal of Honor: [3]

> Michael A. McGann, 1st Sgt.
> Joseph Robinson, 1st Sgt.
> John H. Shingle, 1st Sgt.
> Elmer A. Snow, Trumpeter

At the entrance of the battlefield there is an excellent brochure that explains the progression of the battle. You can drive through the actual battlefield on a good dirt road. You can also hike to several areas on this battlefield just like the infantry did in 1876 (minus the shooting). There is an ancient Buffalo Jump on the battlefield and pictograph drawings on the rocks at the bottom of the jump. Just beyond the Buffalo Jump and a bit north, in the saddle, is where legend has it the Cheyenne girl rescued her brother.

The picture top right is a monument stone. Picture on top left is the gap the Indians rode down at the start of the battle.

Top left picture is the view of battlefield looking south, picture on right is from Headquarters Hill at monument looking West towards Little Big Horn.

Chapter 14

Two Moon Cairn and Memorial

Two Moon Cairn just off Highway 212

R. KENT MORGAN

Two Moon Cairn and Memorial

Other Names: Indian Name Ishi' eyo Nissi
Location: On Highway 212 driving west at Busby Trading Post or General Store, a two story wooden teepee

GPS Position: 45o   31.876N X 106o 57.436W, Elev. 3458' on highway

Note: If you have just been to the Rosebud Battlefield, heading north on Route #314 you will run into highway 212. Take a right turn and you can see Busby not more than a quarter mile off.

Campaign: Followed Crazy Horse's band of Oglalas until they surrendered.
Date: Two Moons died quietly at his home in 1917 [1]
Principal Commanders: None
Forces Engaged: None
Casualties: None

Busby was the last 7th Calvary campsite before the Battle of the Little Big Horn.

Chief Two Moons was one of the principal Northern Cheyenne Chiefs that participated in the battle of the Little Big Horn. He surrendered to Colonel Nelson Miles at Fort Keogh on April 22, 1877, and later became a scout for the Army to help subdue the remaining hostile Sioux and Nez Perce. His body is buried here along with his personal effects and some documents. A few years ago his cairn was broken into and some items were pilfered, but his body still rests within.

Interesting Note: Two Moons distinguished profile would later appear on the famous buffalo nickel. [1]

On the same hill as the Two Moons Cairn and Memorial are buried some twenty four other Indians. These graves bear the identification "Unknown" on small, 3" x 5" aluminum markers, and form a circle, which represents the Cheyenne tradition of the Circle of Life. During the Indian Wars, the government wanted to study Indian remains, so these eventually ended up at the Smithsonian Institute until the tribes gained their release for re-interment, and the remains were repatriated from the Smithsonian in 1933 for reburial at this location.

---

1.   Chiaventone, A Road We Do Not Know, p. 332

Chapter 15

Little Bighorn Battlefield

Last Stand Hill, with Little Bighorn River to the left, and National Cemetery to the right. The dark faced stone in the center is where Custer fell.

R. KENT MORGAN

Little Bighorn Battlefield

Other Names: Custer's Last Stand, Custer's Battlefield, and Indians called it Battle of the Greasy Grass

Location: On I-90 and I-94, 12 miles east of Hardin (well noted on maps and road signs)

Campaign: Yellowstone Expedition

Date: June 25 – 27, 1876

Principal Commanders: Brigadier General Alfred Howe Terry, Commander of the Department of the Dakota (included present-day Minnesota, South and North Dakota and Montana), attached to Terry's command was Lt. Col. George A. Custer, Commander of 7th Cavalry.

Crazy Horse, (Oglala Sioux), Two Moon, (Northern Cheyenne), Gall, (Hunkpapa Sioux) and Sitting Bull, (Hunkpapa Sioux, Medicine Man)

Forces Engaged: 12 companies (647 Men) of the 7th Cavalry
Approximately 4,000 warriors

Casualties: Troops killed - 268 (including several that died of wounds)
Indians killed -100 (including several that died of wounds)

Fought on June 25 to 27, 1876 between Lieutenant Colonel George A. Custer and Confederated Sioux. Several War Chiefs were involved, most notably, Crazy Horse, Gall and Two Moon.

This battlefield is the most well known of the American Indian Campaigns. There are three major reasons why it is so well known:

1.   It was the largest defeat of troops during the Indian wars.
2.   It happened just prior to the 100th Anniversary of the Independence of the United States.
3.   That Lt. Colonel Custer was a very well known personality at this time.

Situated at this site is a beautiful National Cemetery, where Major (Brevet Brigadier General) Marcus Reno is buried who is (highest ranking officer in the cemetery), along with most of Custer's Crow Scouts. Also, the re-interred remains of the men of Fort Kearney, from nearby Buffalo, Wyoming and from Fort C.F. Smith, which is south of Billings, Montana. Also buried here are the remains of troopers found after their initial burial on the battlefield and had been listed as "Unknown Soldiers", but to God. There are also veterans of World Wars I and II, as well as the Korean and Viet Nam wars.

The museum and video on site are worthy of seeing, plus you can hear an excellent lecture by one of the park rangers.

A black top road will take you to the Last Stand Hill and Monument upon which five companies (210 men) of the 7th Cavalry were engaged, under overwhelming odds, with the Indians, which resulted in their deaths. There is a new and very moving Indian Memorial nearby commemorating those warriors that died during this engagement. It is very worthwhile visiting.

Continue on the road approximately four miles to see the location of Major Reno and Captain Benteen's defensive position where they and their gallant troopers held off countless attacks by the Indians over a two-day period. Imagine for a moment while you are visiting, the conditions these men endured at the time: the temperature is over one hundred degrees. Thousands of Indians are firing on you, and you have nothing but a hunting knife or your hands to dig a slit trench into this very hard, rocky soil to provide minimal protection.

There were 24 well-deserved Medals of Honor awarded during this action. Most were attributed to men who ran a gauntlet of Indian fire to obtain water for the wounded, and for providing supporting fire to protect those retrieving water from the Little Big Horn River. Three of these Medals are displayed in the Little Big Horn Museum.

Major Reno and Captain Benteen recommended 24 men to receive the Medal of Honor. They are as follows: [1]

Bancroft, Neil (Pvt. Co. A)#
Brant, Abram B. (Pvt. Co. D)#
Callan, Thomas J. (Pvt. Co. B)#
Criswell, Benjamin (Sgt. Co. B)$
Cunningham, Charles (Cpl. Co. B)+
Deetline, Frederick (Pvt. Co. D)#
Gieger, George (Sgt. Co. H)*
Goldin, Theodore W. (Pvt .Co. G)#
Hanley, Richard P. (Sgt. Co. C)@
Harris, David W. (Pvt. Co. A)#
Harris, William M. (Pvt. Co. D)#
Holden, Henry (Pvt. Co. D)%
Hutchinson, Rufus D. (Sgt. Co. B)#
Mechlin, Henry W.B. Blacksmith, Co. H)*
Murray, Thomas (Sgt. Co. B) ^
Pym, James (Pvt. Co. B)#
Ray, Stanislaus (Sgt. Co. A)#
Scott, George (Pvt. Co. D)#
Stivers, Thomas W. (Pvt. Co. D)#
Thompson, Peter (Pvt. Co. C)#
Tolan, Frank (Pvt. Co. D)#
Voit, Otto (Saddler, Co. H)*
Welch, Charles H. (Sgt. Co. D)#
Windolph, Charles (Pvt. Co. H)*

\#   Volunteered to descend the ravine, through Indian fire, to the Little Big Horn River to obtain water for the wounded.

*   Volunteered, while in exposed positions, to lay down covering fire for those obtaining water for the wounded.

$ Rescued the body of Lieutenant. B. H. Hodgson from within enemy's lines; brought up ammunition and encouraged the men that were in the most exposed positions under heavy fire.

\+   Declined to leave the line when wounded in the neck during heavy fire, and fought bravely all the next day.

@   Single-handedly and without orders recaptured a stampeded pack mule train loaded with ammunition while within enemy lines and under galling fire lasting some 20 minutes.

^   Brought up the pack train, and on the second day, the rations, under heavy fire from the enemy.

%   Brought up ammunition under a galling fire from the enemy. [1]

After Brigadier General Alfred Terry and Colonel John Gibbons discovered the tragedy at the Little Big Horn, Terry ordered the bodies to be buried on June 27,1876. They were mostly covered with a bit dirt and brush, and some attempt was made to identify the terribly mutilated and rapidly decomposing corpses. Wolves and coyotes had dug up the shallow graves and scattered the bones, so it was not until several months later that those officers that could be identified were shipped back to relatives for reburial.

Most of the 200 enlisted troopers were eventually reburied in a common grave under the large memorial stone on the Last Stand Hill. Some were reburied where they had been seen scattered upon the battlefield. The remains of what was believed to be Lt. Colonel George A. Custer was reburied at West Point with his wife Elisabeth.

Captain Tom Custer and most of the officers are buried at Fort Leavenworth, Kansas.

General Terry had expected to meet General Crook and coordinate a consolidated attack on the Indians. Unable to locate Crook, he sent two mounted volunteers carrying dispatches to Crook from Fort Pease. Terry recommended these two volunteers, Pvt. William Evans and Pvt. Benjamin F, Stewart, for the Medal of Honor for carrying dispatches through hostile Indian territory to Crook, who was at Goose Creek, near present-day Sheridan, Wyoming. [1]

Note: Hundreds of books and articles have been written about the Battle of the Little Bighorn, both pro and con. The author encourages you to read and decide for yourself the controversy that still persists today regarding Custer's decision to attack the Indians. There are also hundreds of websites from which to obtain information on the American Indian Wars.

1. Website: **www.army.mil/cmh-pg/mohind.htm** Information about the Medal of Honor during Indian War Period.

Chapter 16

Fort Custer and Hardin

Other Names: Bighorn Post [1]
Located: Drive east on I-90 from Harden and exit on Route 47. Take a left turn on Route 384 on Frontage Road, which runs parallel to the railroad tracks going east, then take the first right turn past the iron railroad bridge. Stay to the right and drive up the winding hill road to the top or butte. You will come upon an immense plateau in front of you; this was the location of the fort.

GPS Position: 45o 43.605N X 107o 34.302W, Elev. 3036' , (overlooking Hardin)

The Campaign: After Colonel Nelson A. Miles' Winter Campaigns
Date: Built during the summer of 1877, abandoned in 1898
Principal Commander: Unknown
Forces Engaged: Troops participated in the Nez Perce Campaign of 1877
Casualties: None

It was established and built in the summer of 1877, at the same time as Fort Keogh in Miles City. Nothing remains except the size of the fort's parade grounds. This fort was occupied for 21 years and closed in 1898.

Named after Lt. Colonel Custer of the 7th Calvary. Colonel Miles, General Sheridan and General Sherman selected this site because it is at the convergence of the Little Big Horn with the Big Horn Rivers.

Special Note: On its anniversary on the fourth weekend in June, there are two living history reenactments of the Little Big Horn Battle outside Harden. Contact: Bighorn County Historical Museum, RR 1, Box 1206A, Hardin, MT 59034-2433, (406) 655-1671 for schedule and details.

Another living history reenactment is at the Little Big Horn Battlefield, next to the actual site. The Real Bird Family of the Crow Tribe produces this reenactment. Contacts are: The Crow Tribal Office, P.O. Box 159, Crow Agency, MT 59022, (406) 638-2601 (Ext. 104 or 222) or Custer Battlefield Trading Post, Putt and Jill Thompson, (406) 638-2270 for schedule and details.

Both living history reenactments are excellent.

---

1.   Greene, Yellowstone Command, p. 224

Chapter 17

Fort C.F. Smith and Hayfield Fight

Pictures are of the memorial plaque for Hayfield Fight in the actual hayfield.

R. KENT MORGAN

Fort C.F. Smith and Hayfield Fight

Other Names: None
Location: From Hardin take Highway 313 south to St. Xavier and continue on 313 (at the Lodge Grass turn-off it is another 12.8 miles on Highway 313) to see the location of the Hay Field Fight. Road signs also indicate the Bighorn Camping and Fishing Camp.

GPS Position: 45o 19.934N X 107o 52.072W, Elev. 3200 turn right off Highway 313.

Note: You will drive down a slight hill, cross over an irrigation canal bridge. On your left side, behind a pine tree, is the Memorial Rock indicating the location of the Hay Field Fight. Hay is still grown in this field.

GPS Position: 45o 20.110N X 107o 52.44W, Elev. 3142 at the Memorial Rock

Campaign: Bozeman Trail in 1866
Date: Built on August 12, 1866; Hayfield Fight August 1, 1867 [1]
Principal Commanders: Lt. Colonel Luther P. Bradley [1]
Chief Red Cloud, Oglala Sioux
Forces Engaged: Sioux
Casualties: Three Troops killed and three wounded [1]
Estimated 50 to 100 Indians killed and wounded [1]

Fort C.F. Smith was established and built in 1866 to protect immigrants, mostly gold miners along the Bozeman Trail, from the attack by the Sioux. There were four military forts along the Bozeman Trail, Fort C.F. Smith, Fort Philip Kearny (near Buffalo, Wyoming), Fort Reno (near Kaycee, Wyoming) and Fort Fetterman (Douglas, Wyoming).

The Bozeman Trail had extended through prime Indian hunting grounds so you can imagine that the Indians didn't care too much for this. These forts were under constant siege by the Indians. The Forts C.F. Smith, Philip Kearny, and Reno were soon abandoned after the Fort Laramie Treaty of 1868. The Indians burned down the forts. Only Fort Fetterman was manned and used until it was abandoned in 1884.

The forts along the Bozeman hired civilian contractors to harvest hay for their livestock, and each fort provided military escorts to guard these contractors. Fort C.F. Smith had hired A.C. Leighton as it's contractor. [1]

On August 1, 1867, twelve contractors were harvesting natural hay two and a half miles away. Lieutenant Sigmund Sternberg, a Civil War Veteran escorted the civilians, along with nineteen infantrymen armed with new breechloading rifles. Due to frequent raids a picket corral had been built for some measure of protection. At around 9:00 AM, an estimated 1000 Indians attacked the infantrymen and civilians. Lt. Sternberg was killed at the opening of the battle. An ex-Army Captain in the Civil War, a contract worker Al Colvin assumed command. He was armed with a 16 shot .44 caliber Henry repeating rifle, and others maintained a constant fire upon the Indians. Around noon a dispatch was sent back to the fort for a relief force that didn't arrive until almost sunset, relieving and escorting the combatants back to the fort.

All that remains of Fort C.F. Smith are some low mounds in the middle of a field.

If you go up to Highway 313 and take a right turn and continue for about two miles at **GPS Position 45o 19.568N X 107o 52.918W, Elev. 3242** on the highway, look at or for a deep ravine on your right side. Where the ravine empties into the Bighorn River to the right of this ravine, now farm area, was the location of Fort C.F. Smith.

Note: The men that died here at this fort have been re-interred at the Custer National Cemetery. The Stone monument in the cemetery is well over 10 feet tall, one of the tallest in the cemetery.

---

1.   O'Neal, Fighting Men of the Indian Wars, p. 92 & 93

Chapter 18

Chief Plenty Coups State Park

R. KENT MORGAN

Chief Plenty Coups State Park

Other Names: Indian Name: A Lek - Chea - Ahoosh
Location: From Fort C.F. Smith drive 21 miles north on Route 313 to St. Xavier; take a left turn to Pryor heading west. Once at Pryor, turn right at the south end of town and Chief Plenty Coups State Park is a short distance to the west. Noted on road signs.

GPS Position: 45o 25.733N X 108o 32.971W, Elev. 4056' at grave site

Campaigns: Scout at the Battle of the Rosebud with General Crook.
Date: Chief Plenty Coups died in 1932
Principal Commanders: Crow Tribe allied with government
Forces Engaged: None
Casualties: None

Chief Plenty Coups State Park is a memorial to a Great Crow Tribe Chief who was a warrior, diplomat, rancher, farmer and proprietor of a general store. Chief Plenty Coups lived on this land, and is buried here at this park with his two wives and a daughter. It has an excellent museum; in addition, his home and dwelling, as well as the medicine spring nearby he visited almost daily are open.

The park is open daily from 8 AM to 8 PM. The museum hours are from 10 AM to 5 PM from May 1st to September 30th. At other times, call for an appointment and to learn about other events. (406) 252-1289.

Chapter 19

Canyon Creek Battle

Picture on left is the canyon were Nez Perce held off the troops picture of plaque by Highway 532.

R. KENT MORGAN

Canyon Creek Battle

Other Names: Canyon Creek Battlefield or Canyon Creek Battle
Location: From Pryor drive west to Edgar, take US Highway 310 north to Laurel, MT. Go north on Highway 532 about 8.3 miles. On the left hand side is a Memorial Stone with a plaque.

GPS Position: 45o 46.564N X 108o 47.791W, Elev. 3441' at plaque

Campaign: Nez Perce Campaign 1877
Date: September 13, 1877
Principal Commanders: Colonel Samuel Davis Sturgis
Chief Looking Glass and Chief Joseph

Forces Engaged: 350 Troops of the 7[1] Cavalry [1]
Estimated 300 Indian warriors [1]
Casualties: Three Troops killed and eleven wounded [1]
Twenty-one Nez Perce killed [1]

The Nez Perce were escaping to Canada from their homeland in Wallowa Valley, Oregon. The Indians had crossed the Yellowstone River and burned a stage station near Laurel Canyon when engaged in a daylong battle with Colonel Sturgis' Cavalry. The Nez Perce delayed the troops long enough for the tribe to escape to the north, then melted away during the night. Colonel Sturgis was widely criticized for his ineffective efforts during the clash and for not following the retreating Indians.

Just sixteen days later, on September 30, 1977, the Nez Perce were halted and defeated by Colonel Nelson Miles at the Bear Paw Mountains, some 30 miles from the Canadian Border. Chief Joseph surrendered to Miles and General Oliver Otis Howard on October 5, 1877.

---

1. O'Neal, Fighting Men of the Indian Wars, p. 209

Appendix # 1

The readers might ask themselves why so many Medals of Honor were awarded?

My explanation is as follows; The Medal of Honor was basically the only medal that could be awarded to both enlisted and officers during these Indian Wars.

The Medal of Honor (Army) was first authorized by Congress on July 12,1862, and was the same as the Navy Medal, authorized a few months earlier with a different suspension. There were 1,520 medals awarded during the Civil War. There were 428 medals awarded during the Indian Wars, all to the Army. Six were awarded posthumously.

The criteria for the Medal of Honor at this time were simply valorous conduct on the field of battle. Most of the 31 Medals awarded to the 5th Infantry under Colonel Nelson Miles simply read: "Gallantry in Engagement or Gallantry in Action". [1]

Having said this, there was another medal that could have been awarded to enlisted personnel (Privates only) called the Certificate of Merit.

The Certificate of Merit was established during the Mexican War by an Act of Congress of March 3, 1847, it was originally a Paper

Certificate, to be awarded by the President to Privates only for gallantry in action, or for special meritorious service in time of peace. Some 545 men received the Certificates of Merit during the Mexican War. It wasn't until January 11, 1905, that a medal was authorized to be worn. Due to the Certificate of Merit limitations it was not awarded in the Indian Wars, leaving only the Medal of Honor.

During the Indian Wars from 1865 to 1891, which commenced immediately following the Civil War, the U.S. Army was engaged in a series of small battles with the Indians over a number of years.

These were from skirmishes to a few pitched battles, but did not compare to the magnitude seen during the Civil War.

For the most part, the Officers and NCOs were combat hardened veterans of the Civil War. The ranks were filled mostly with new immigrants, some of whom had fought in the Civil War. Most joined because of the economic conditions following the Civil War. The Indians called them either Horse Soldiers or Long Knives(Cavalry) or Walk-a-Heaps (Infantry).

Troops were engaged throughout this period, yet the Indian's Campaigns were third page news until June 25, 1876, when tragic news of Battle at the Little Bighorn became front page news.

Congress did not recognize the Indian Wars until March 1890, when they recognized the troops as "Veterans" in a sense that they campaigned against an armed enemy of the United States.

Appendix # 2

What became of these Officers and other notables that were directly involved in the Indian wars?

President Ulysses Simpson Grant, Born 4-27-1822, Died 7-23-1885, President (1869-77), Civil War Lt. General, and West Point graduate. After the presidency entered business on Wall Street and lost all his money. Wrote magazine articles about his military life, diagnosed with cancer in 1884, wrote his autobiography and finished it right before his death. The sales from the book restored his family's wealth. Buried at General Grant's National Memorial, New York City.

Lieutenant General William Tecumseh Sherman, Born 2-8-1820, Died 2-14-1891, Civil War Lt. General and West Point graduate. Known for his march through Georgia to the sea during the Civil War. Became General of the Army after the Civil War during Grant's Administration. Buried at Calvary Cemetery, St. Louis, Missouri.

Major General Philip Henry Sheridan Sr., Born 3-6-1831, Died 9-5-1888 in Chicago, Illinois. A West Point graduate and Lt. General of the Army, who replaced William T. Sherman after retirement. Buried at Arlington National Cemetery.

Brigadier General George Crook, Born 9-80-1830, Died 3-21-1890 in Chicago, Illinois. West Point graduate and Major General in command of the Department of the Missouri. Buried at Arlington National Cemetery.

Brigadier General Alfred H. Terry, Born 7-28-1832, Died 12-16-1890, Harvard graduate, promoted to Major General in 1886, Commander of the Missouri, retired on disability 1888. Buried Grove Street Burial Ground, New Haven, CT.

Lieutenant Colonel George A. Custer, Born 12-5-1839, Died 6-25-1876, West Point graduate, one of the boy Major Generals in Civil War. After war demoted to Lt. Colonel. Died at Little Bighorn, buried with his wife at West Point, New York.

Major Marcus A. Reno, Born 11-15-1834, Died 4-1-89, West Point graduate, promoted to Brigadier General in Civil War. Later dismissed from Army for "prejudicial to the good order and discipline" and died on 4-1-1889 in Washington, DC. Re-interred to Custer National Cemetery in Montana, with full military honors, the highest ranking officer in the cemetery, in 1967.

Captain Frederick W. Benteen, Born 8-24-1834, Died 6-22-1898, Civil War Veteran. Participated in the Battle at Canyon Creek against Nez Perce. Rose to the rank of Brig. General in 1890. Died in Atlanta and is buried at Arlington National Cemetery.

Captain Thomas Benton Weir, Born 9-28-1838, Died 12-9-1876, graduated from University of Michigan in 1861, Civil War Veteran, served with the 7th Cavalry assigned to Major Reno's command at Little Bighorn. He attempted to rescue Custer, but was turned back by the Indians. His furthest point of advance is noted as "Weir's Point" at Little Big Horn Battlefield. He died in New York City, buried at Cypress Hills National Cemetery, Brooklyn, NY.

Colonel William Babcock Hazen, Born 9-27-1830, Died 1-16-1887, West Point graduate, Commander at Fort Buford during 1876 and 1877 Indian Wars. Later appointed by President Hayes a Chief Signal Officer as a Brigadier General.

Buried at Arlington National Cemetery.

Colonel Nelson A. Miles, Born 8-8-1839, Died 5-15-1925, One of the boy Major Generals in Civil War, awarded Medal of Honor for gallantry at Chancellorsville during the Civil War. After war demoted to Colonel, promoted to Brigadier General in 1880, promoted to Major General in 1890 replaced General John M. Schofield as Army's Command-in-Chief 10-5-1895, promoted to Lt. General in 1901. Took mandatory retirement in 1903. Died of a heart attack while standing during the National Anthem with his grandchildren at a circus. Buried at Arlington National Cemetery.

Lieutenant Frank D. Baldwin, Born 6-26-1842, Died 4-22-1923, awarded Medal of Honor in Civil War and Second Medal of Honor in Indian Wars for rescuing two captive girls. Fought in Spanish-American War. Promoted to Brigadier General in 1902. Retired from active duty 6-26-1906. Promoted to Major General in 1915. Died in Denver, buried at Arlington National Cemetery about 40 yards away from General Nelson A. Miles.

Colonel Elwell Stephen Otis, Born 3-25-1838, Died 10-21-1909, lawyer before the war. Promoted to Major General on June 16, 1906, led troops in the Spanish American War and became Military Governor of the Philippine Islands from 1898 to 1900. Buried at Arlington National Cemetery.

First Lieutenant George W. Baird, Born 12-13-1839, Died 11-28-1906, Medal of Honor recipient and received Medal in 1894, Citation reads, "Most distinguished gallantry in action with Nez Perce Indians". He was Col. Miles' Adjutant (from 1871 to 1879). He was severely wounded at the Bear Paw Mountains on 9-30-1877. Baird rose from a private during the Civil War to Brigadier General. He published accounts of Miles' campaigns and several officers. In 1879 he transferred to the Pay Department because of the wound received at Bear Paw, and retired in 1903. Buried at Milford Cemetery, Milford, New Haven County, Connecticut.

Capt. Simon Snyder, served in the 5th Infantry almost continuously from 1861 to1888. He participated in the Fort Peck Expedition and later headed the mounted infantry detachment organized toward the end of the Sioux War. After a career spanning the Civil, Indian, and Spanish-American Wars, he retired as a Brigadier General in 1902. His diaries are an excellent and important resource.

Second Lieutenant James Worden Pope, Born 6-6-1846, Died 8-23-1919, West Point graduate of 1868, wrote eyewitness account of the Cedar Creek battle. At Wolf Mts. Battle commanded two artillery pieces. Later commanded U.S. Military Prison at Fort Leavenworth, and as Chief Quartermaster of the expeditionary force to the Philippines in 1898. Pope retired as a Brigadier General in 1916 and died in Denver. Buried at Arlington National Cemetery.

First Lieutenant Mason Carter, Born 1834, Died1909, Civil War veteran and Medal of Honor recipient as a 1st LT leading a charge under fire during the Nez Perce Indian Campaigns at Bear Paw Mountain in 1877. He rose to the rank of Major in the Army. Died in California and buried at Fort Rosecrans National Cemetery in California. He was the first Medal of Honor recipient to be interned.

Captain Edmond Butler, Born 9-19-1827, Died 8-24-1895, received the Medal of Honor on 11-27-94, citation reads "Most Distinguished Gallantry in action against Hostile Indians" for his efforts on January 18, 1877 at the Battle of Wolf Mountain. He rose to the rank of Lt. Colonel. Died in Omaha, buried Holy Sepulcher Cemetery, Omaha, Nebraska.

First Lieutenant Robert McDonald, Born 5-12-1822, Died 5-20-1901, received Medal of Honor for January 18, 1877 Battle of Wolf Mountain. Medal was issued on 11-27-1894. Died in Alameda County, CA, buried Lone Tree Cemetery, Hayward, California.

Captain James S. Casey, Born Philadelphia, Pennsylvania, received Medal of Honor for January 18, 1877 Battle of Wolf Mountain. Medal was issued on 11-27-1894. Rose to Colonel and commander of the 22nd Infantry from January 1895 – January 1897.

Most of the Officers that died at the Little Bighorn are buried at Fort Leavenworth, Kansas. They include Keogh, Tom Custer, Yates, Smith, Calhoun, Harrington, Crittenden, Porter, Sturgis and Dr. Lord. Lt. Cook is buried in Hamilton Cemetery, Ontario, Canada.

Appendix # 3

FORT LARAMIE TREADY 1868
ARTICLES OF A TREATY MADE AND CONCLUDED
BY AND BETWEEN

Lieutenant General William T. Sherman, General William S. Harney, General Alfred H. Terry, General O. O. Augur, J. B. Henderson, Nathaniel G. Taylor, John G. Sanborn, and Samuel F. Tappan, duly appointed commissioners on the part of the United States, and the different bands of the Sioux Nation of Indians, by their chiefs and headmen, whose names are hereto subscribed, they being duly authorized to act in the premises.

ARTICLE I.
From this day forward all war between the parties to this agreement shall for ever cease. The government of the United States desires peace, and its honor is hereby pledged to keep it. The Indians desire peace, and they now pledge their honor to maintain it.

If bad men among the whites, or among other people subject to the authority of the United States, shall commit any wrong upon the person or property of the Indians, the United States will, upon proof made to the agent, and forwarded to the Commissioner of Indian Affairs at Washington city, proceed at once to cause the offender to be arrested and punished according to the laws of the United States, and also reimburse the injured person for the loss sustained.

If bad men among the Indians shall commit a wrong or depredation upon the person or property of nay one, white, black, or Indian, subject to the authority of the United States, and at peace therewith, the Indians herein named solemnly agree that they will, upon proof made to their agent, and notice by him, deliver up the wrongdoer to the United States, to be tried and punished according to its laws, and, in case they willfully refuse so to do, the person injured shall be reimbursed for his loss from the annuities, or other moneys due or to become due to them under this or other treaties made with the United States; and the President, on advising with the Commissioner of Indian Affairs, shall prescribe such rules and regulations for ascertaining damages under the provisions of this article as in his judgment may be proper, but no one sustaining loss while violating the provisions of this treaty, or the laws of the United States, shall be reimbursed therefore.

ARTICLE II.

The United States agrees that the following district of country, to wit, viz: commencing on the east bank of the Missouri river where the 46th parallel of north latitude crosses the same, thence along low-water mark down said east bank to a point opposite where the northern line of the State of Nebraska strikes the river, thence west across said river, and along the northern line of Nebraska to the 104th degree of longitude west from Greenwich, thence north on said meridian to a point where the 46th parallel of north latitude intercepts the same, thence due east along said parallel to the place of beginning; and in addition thereto, all existing reservations of the east back of said river, shall be and the same is, set apart for the absolute and undisturbed use and occupation of the Indians herein named, and for such other friendly tribes or individual Indians as from time to time they may be willing, with the consent of the United States, to admit amongst them; and the United States now solemnly agrees that no persons, except those herein designated and authorized so to do, and except such officers, agents, and employees of the government as may be authorized to enter upon Indian reservations in discharge of duties enjoined by law, shall ever be permitted to pass over, settle upon, or reside in the territory described in this article, or in such territory as may be added to this reservation for the use of said Indians, and henceforth they will and do hereby relinquish all claims or right in and to any portion of the United States or Territories, except such as is embraced within the limits aforesaid, and except as hereinafter provided.

ARTICLE III.

If it should appear from actual survey or other satisfactory examination of said tract of land that it contains less than 160 acres of tillable land for each person who, at the time, may be authorized to reside on it under the provisions of this treaty, and a very considerable number of such persons shall be disposed to commence cultivating the soil as farmers, the United States agrees to set apart, for the use of said Indians, as herein provided, such additional quantity of arable land, adjoining to said reservation, or as near to the same as it can be obtained, as may be required to provide the necessary amount.

ARTICLE IV.

The United States agrees, at its own proper expense, to construct, at some place on the Missouri river, near the center of said reservation where timber and water may be convenient, the following buildings, to wit, a warehouse, a store-room for the use of the agent in storing goods belonging to the Indians, to cost not less than $2,500; an agency building, for the residence of the agent, to cost not exceeding $3,000; a residence for the physician, to cost not more than $3,000; and five other buildings, for a carpenter, farmer, blacksmith, miller, and engineer-each to cost not exceeding $2,000; also, a school-house, or mission building, so soon as a sufficient number of children can be induced by the agent to attend school, which shall not cost exceeding $5,000.

The United States agrees further to cause to be erected on said reservation, near the other buildings herein authorized, a good steam circular saw-mill, with a grist-mill and shingle machine attached to the same, to cost not exceeding $8,000.

ARTICLE V.

The United States agrees that the agent for said Indians shall in the future make his home at the agency building; that he shall reside among them, and keep an office open at all times for the purpose of prompt and diligent inquiry into such matters of complaint by and against the Indians as may be presented for investigation under the provisions of their treaty stipulations, as also for the faithful discharge of other duties enjoined on him by law. In all cases of depredation on person or property he shall cause the evidence to be taken in writing and forwarded, together with his findings, to the Commissioner of Indian Affairs, whose decision, subject to the revision of the Secretary of the Interior, shall be binding on the parties to this treaty.

ARTICLE VI.

If any individual belonging to said tribes of Indians, or legally incorporated with them, being the head of a family, shall desire to commence farming, he shall have the privilege to select, in the presence and with the assistance of the agent then in charge, a tract of land within said reservation, not exceeding three hundred and twenty acres in extent, which tract, when so selected, certified, and recorded in the "Land Book" as herein directed, shall cease to be held in common, but the same may be occupied and held in the exclusive possession of the person selecting it, and of his family, so long as he or they may continue to cultivate it.

Any person over eighteen years of age, not being the head of a family, may in like manner select and cause to be certified to him or her, for purposes of cultivation, a quantity of land, not exceeding eighty acres in extent, and thereupon be entitled to the exclusive possession of the same as above directed.
For each tract of land so selected a certificate, containing a description thereof and the name of the person selecting it, with a certificate endorsed thereon that the same has been recorded, shall be delivered to the party entitled to it, by the agent, after the same shall have been recorded by him in a book to be kept in his office, subject to inspection, which said book shall be known as the "Sioux Land Book."

The President may, at any time, order a survey of the reservation, and, when so surveyed, Congress shall provide for protecting the rights of said settlers in their improvements, and may fix the character of the title held by each. The United States may pass such laws on the subject of alienation and descent of property between the Indians and their descendants as may be thought proper. And it is further stipulated that any male Indians over eighteen years of age, of any band or tribe that is or shall hereafter become a party to this treaty, who now is or who shall hereafter become a resident or occupant of any reservation or territory not included in the tract of country designated and described in this treaty for the permanent home of the Indians, which is not mineral land, nor reserved by the United States for special purposes other than Indian occupation, and who shall have made improvements thereon of the value of two hundred dollars or more, and continuously occupied the same as a homestead for the term of three years, shall be entitled to receive from the United States a patent for one hundred and sixty acres of land including his said improvements, the same to be in the form of the legal subdivisions of the surveys of the public lands. Upon application in writing, sustained by the proof of two disinterested witnesses, made to the register of the local land office when the land sought to be entered is within a land district, and when the tract sought to be entered is not in any land district, then upon said application and proof being made to the Commissioner of the General Land Office, and the right of such Indian or Indians to enter such tract or tracts of land shall accrue and be perfect from the date of his first improvements thereon, and shall continue as long as be continues his residence and improvements and no longer. And any Indian or Indians receiving a patent for land under the foregoing provisions shall thereby and from thenceforth become and be a citizen of the United States and be entitled to all the privileges and immunities of such citizens, and shall, at the same time, retain all his rights to benefits accruing to Indians under this treaty.

ARTICLE VII.

In order to insure the civilization of the Indians entering into this treaty, the necessity of education is admitted, especially of such of them as are or may be settled on said agricultural reservations, and they, therefore, pledge themselves to compel their children, male and female, between the ages of six and sixteen years, to attend school, and it is hereby made the duty of the agent for said Indians to see that this stipulation is strictly complied with; and the United States agrees that for every thirty children between said ages, who can be induced or compelled to attend school, a house shall be provided, and a teacher competent to teach the elementary branches of an English education shall be furnished, who will reside among said Indians and faithfully discharge his or her duties as a teacher. The provisions of this article to continue for not less than twenty years.

ARTICLE VIII.

When the head of a family or lodge shall have selected lands and received his certificate as above directed, and the agent shall be satisfied that he intends in good faith to commence cultivating the soil for a living, he shall be entitled to receive seeds and agricultural implements for the first year, not exceeding in value one hundred dollars, and for each succeeding year he shall continue to farm, for a period of three years more, he shall be entitled to receive seeds and implements as aforesaid, not exceeding in value twenty-five dollars. And it is further stipulated that such persons as commence farming shall receive instruction from the farmer herein provided for, and whenever more than one hundred persons shall enter upon the cultivation of the soil, a second blacksmith shall be provided, with such iron, steel, and other material as may be needed.

ARTICLE IX.

At any time after ten years from the making of this treaty, the United States shall have the privilege of withdrawing the physician, farmer, blacksmith, carpenter, engineer, and miller herein provided for, but in case of such withdrawal, an additional sum thereafter of ten thousand dollars per annum shall be devoted to the education of said Indians, and the Commissioner of Indian Affairs shall, upon careful inquiry into their condition, make such rules and regulations for the expenditure of said sums as will best promote the education and moral improvement of said tribes.

ARTICLE X.

In lieu of all sums of money or other annuities provided to be paid to the Indians herein named under any treaty or treaties heretofore made, the United States agrees to deliver at the agency house on the reservation herein named, on or before the first day of August of each year, for thirty years, the following articles, to wit:
For each male person over 14 years of age, a suit of good substantial woolen clothing, consisting of coat, pantaloons, flannel shirt, hat, and a pair of home-made socks.

For each female over 12 years of age, a flannel shirt, or the goods necessary to make it, a pair of woolen hose, 12 yards of calico, and 12 yards of cotton domestics.

For the boys and girls under the ages named, such flannel and cotton goods as may be needed to make each a suit as aforesaid, together with a pair of woolen hose for each.

And in order that the Commissioner of Indian Affairs may be able to estimate properly for the articles herein named, it shall be the duty of the agent each year to forward to him a full and exact census of the Indians, on which the estimate from year to year can be based.

And in addition to the clothing herein named, the sum of $10 for each person entitled to the beneficial effects of this treaty shall be annually appropriated for a period of 30 years, while such persons roam and hunt, and $20 for each person who engages in farming, to be used by the Secretary of the Interior in the purchase of such articles as from time to time the condition and necessities of the Indians may indicate to be proper. And if within the 30 years, at any time, it shall appear that the amount of money needed for clothing, under this article, can be appropriated to better uses for the Indians named herein, Congress may, by law, change the appropriation to other purposes, but in no event shall the amount of the appropriation be withdrawn or discontinued for the period named. And the President shall annually detail an officer of the army to be present and attest the delivery of all the goods herein named, to the Indians, and he shall inspect and report on the quantity and quality of the goods and the manner of their delivery.

And it is hereby expressly stipulated that each Indian over the age of four years, who shall have removed to and settled permanently upon said reservation, one pound of meat and one pound of flour per day, provided the Indians cannot furnish their own subsistence at an earlier date. And it is further stipulated that the United States will furnish and deliver to each lodge of Indians or family of persons legally incorporated with the, who shall remove to the reservation herein described and commence farming, one good American cow, and one good well-broken pair of American oxen within 60 days after such lodge or family shall have so settled upon said reservation.

ARTICLE XI.

In consideration of the advantages and benefits conferred by this treaty and the many pledges of friendship by the United States, the tribes who are parties to this agreement hereby stipulate that they will relinquish all right to occupy permanently the territory outside their reservations as herein defined, but yet reserve the right to hunt on any lands north of North Platte, and on the Republican Fork of the Smoky Hill river, so long as the buffalo may range thereon in such numbers as to justify the chase. And they, the said Indians, further expressly agree:

1st. That they will withdraw all opposition to the construction of the railroads now being built on the plains.

2d. That they will permit the peaceful construction of any railroad not passing over their reservation as herein defined.

3d. That they will not attack any persons at home, or traveling, nor molest or disturb any wagon trains, coaches, mules, or cattle belonging to the people of the United States, or to persons friendly therewith.

4th. They will never capture, or carry off from the settlements, white women or children.

5th. They will never kill or scalp white men, nor attempt to do them harm.

6th. They withdraw all pretence of opposition to the construction of the railroad now being built along the Platte river and westward to the Pacific ocean, and they will not in future object to the construction of railroads, wagon roads, mail stations, or other works of utility or necessity, which may be ordered or permitted by the laws of the United States. But should such roads or other works be constructed on the lands of their reservation, the government will pay the tribe whatever amount of damage may be assessed by three disinterested commissioners to be appointed by the President for that purpose, one of the said commissioners to be a chief or headman of the tribe.

7th. They agree to withdraw all opposition to the military posts or roads now established south of the North Platte river, or that may be established, not in violation of treaties heretofore made or hereafter to be made with any of the Indian tribes.

ARTICLE XII.

No treaty for the cession of any portion or part of the reservation herein described which may be held in common, shall be of any validity or force as against the said Indians unless executed and signed by at least three-fourths of all the adult male Indians occupying or interested in the same, and no cession by the tribe shall be understood or construed in such manner as to deprive, without his consent, any individual member of the tribe of his rights to any tract of land selected by him as provided in **Article VI** of this treaty.

ARTICLE XIII.

The United States hereby agrees to furnish annually to the Indians the physician, teachers, carpenter, miller, engineer, farmer, and blacksmiths, as herein contemplated, and that such appropriations shall be made from time to time, on the estimate of the Secretary of the Interior, as will be sufficient to employ such persons.

ARTICLE XIV.

It is agreed that the sum of five hundred dollars annually for three years from date shall be expended in presents to the ten persons of said tribe who in the judgment of the agent may grow the most valuable crops for the respective year.

ARTICLE XV.

The Indians herein named agree that when the agency house and other buildings shall be constructed on the reservation named, they will regard said reservation their permanent home, and they will make no permanent settlement elsewhere; but they shall have the right, subject to the conditions and modifications of this treaty, to hunt, as stipulated in **Article XI** hereof.

ARTICLE XVI.

The United States hereby agrees and stipulates that the country north of the North Platte river and east of the summits of the Big Horn mountains shall be held and considered to be unceded. Indian territory, and also stipulates and agrees that no white person or persons shall be permitted to settle upon or occupy any portion of the same; or without the consent of the Indians, first had and obtained, to pass through the same; and it is further agreed by the United States, that within ninety days after the conclusion of peace with all the bands of the Sioux nation, the military posts now established in the territory in this article named shall be abandoned, and that the road leading to them and by them to the settlements in the Territory of Montana shall be closed.

ARTICLE XVII.

It is hereby expressly understood and agreed by and between the respective parties to this treaty that the execution of this treaty and its ratification by the United States Senate shall have the effect, and shall be construed as abrogating and annulling all treaties and agreements heretofore entered into between the respective parties hereto, so far as such treaties and agreements obligate the United States to furnish and provide money, clothing, or other articles of property to such Indians and bands of Indians as become parties to this treaty, but no further.

In testimony of all which, we, the said commissioners, and we, the chiefs and headmen of the Brule band of the Sioux nation, have hereunto set our hands and seals at Fort Laramie, Dakota Territory, this twenty-ninth day of April, in the year one thousand eight hundred and sixty-eight.

Signed by 8 Government Officials including 4 General Officers
Signed by 25 Brule Sioux Band Chief's on April 29, 168
Signed by 38 Oglala Sioux Band Chief's on May 25, 1868
Signed by 16 Minneconjou Sioux Band Chief's on May 25, 1868
Signed by 22 Yanctonais Sioux Band Chief' on May 25,1868
Signed by 26 Arapahoes Chief's on May 25, 1868
Signed by 6 Sioux Reservation Chief's on November 6, 1868

Appendix # 4

The War Department General Order No. 12 established Indian Wars Medal on January 21, 1907 some 42 years after the Indian Wars began.

The Indian Campaign Medals were awarded for military service against any tribes or in any areas listed below during 1865 to 1891: The ribbon is Red with two vertical Blue strips on each side, the face of the medal has a mounted Indian Chief with a lance. Indian Wars is cast above the Indian. On the reverse is cast the American Eagle with United State Army above the Eagle and For Service cast under the Eagle.

Indian Campaigns as follows:

- Southern Oregon, Idaho, Northern California, and Nevada between 1865 to 1875.
- Comanche's and confederated tribes in Kansas, Colorado, Texas,
- New Mexico, and Indian Territory between 1867 to 1875.
- Modoc War (Northern California, and Southern Oregon) 1872 to 1873.
- Apaches in Arizona in 1873.
- Northern Cheyenne and Sioux in 1876 to 1877.
- Nez Perce War in 1877.
- Bannock War in 1878.

- Northern Cheyenne in 1878 to 1879.
- Sheep-Eaters, Piutes, and Bannocks between June and October 1879.
- Utes in Colorado and Utah between September 1879 and
- November 1880.
- Apaches in Arizona and New Mexico in 1885 to January 1891.
- Sioux in South Dakota between November 1890 to January 1891.

Bibliography

Books

Capps, Benjamin. *The Indians*: Time-Life Book series, Pictures and Text: New York: Time Inc., 1973.

Chiaventone, Fredrick J. *A Road We Do Not Know*: A novel of Custer at the Little Bighorn: New York: Simon & Schuster, 1996.

Dillon, Richard H. *Indian Wars 1850-1890*: Indian battles from 1850-1890: New York: Exeter Books, 1984.

Greene, Jerome A. *Yellowstone Command*: Colonel Nelson A. Miles and the Great Sioux War, 1876-1877: Lincoln: University of Nebraska Press, 1991.

Grinnell, George Bird. *The Fighting Cheyennes*: The wars of the Cheyennes, Vol. 44 in The Civilization of the American Indian Series: New Haven: University of Oklahoma Press, 1915.

Hedren, Paul L. *Traveler's Guide to the Great Sioux War*: The battlefields, forts, and related sites of America's greatest Indian war: Helena: Montana Historical Society Press, 1996.

Johnson, Virginia W. *The Unregimented General*: A Biography of Nelson A. Miles: Boston: Houghton Mifflin Company, 1962.

Johnston, Terry C. *Plainsmen Novels*: Series of Books 1-14, covering battles from 1866 to 1877: New York: St. Martin's Press, 1990-1999.

Miles, Nelson A. *Personal Recollections & Observation of General Nelson A. Miles:* Miles' personal recollections: Chicago: Werner and Co., 1896.

McDermott, John D. A *Guide to the Indian Wars of the West*: A descriptive analysis of more than a hundred sites in the west: Lincoln: University of Nebraska Press, 1998.

National Park Service. *Soldier and Brave*: Indian and Military affairs in the Trans-Mississippi West, Including a Guide to Historical Sites and Landmarks Vol. XII: New York: Harper & Row, 1963.

O'Neal, Bill. *Fighting Men of the Indian Wars*: A Biographical Encyclopedia of the Mountain Men, Soldiers, Cowboys, and Pioneers who took up arms during American's Westward Expansion: Stillwell: Barbed Wire Press, 1991.

Nevin, David. *The Soldiers*: Time-Life Books series, Pictures and Text: New York: Time Inc, 1973.

Overfield, Loyd J. II. *The Little Big Horn 1876*: The Official Communications, Documents and Reports with Rosters of the Officers and Troops of the Campaign: Lincoln: University of Nebraska Press, 1971.

Quaife, M.M. *Yellowstone Kelly*: The memoirs of Luther S. Kelly: Lincoln: University of Nebraska Press, 1926.

Steinbach, Robert H. *A Long March:* The Lives of Frank and Alice Baldwin: Austin: University of Texas Press, 1989.

Utley, Robert M. *The Lance and The Shield*: The Life and Times of Sitting Bull: New York: Henry Holt and Co., 1993., *Encyclopedia of the American West*: An A to Z format, portraits of various group of people in the West: New York: Wings Books, 1997., *The Indian Frontier of the American West 1846-1890*: Histories of the American Frontier: Albuquerque: University of New Mexico, 1984.

Vaughn, J. W. *With Crook at the Rosebud:* Description in detail of the battle at the Rosebud 2 Vol.: Harrisburg: Stackpole Books, 1956.

Website Articles

Indian War Period Medals of Honor –
www.army.mil/cmh-pg/mohind.htm Provides all the Recipients Names, Ranks, Organization, Place and Dates of Action, Where men entered the service at, Date Medal was issued and Citation description.

Medal of Honor Statistics –
www.army.mil/cmh-pg/mohstats.htm Provides the Medal of Honor Breakdown by Action, total number issued to which branch of service.

Information on Travel –
www.visitmt.com - Is an excellent site and information on touring Montana.

Information through **www.yahoo.com** - Miscellaneous Items as follows; Little Big Horn, Major Reno's Report on Little Big Horn, Terry's Official Report on the Little Big Horn Disaster, Benteen's Official Report, 4 July 1876, George A. Custer, literally 1000's on hits regarding the histories of the Indian Campaigns, battles, the warriors and soldiers that fought them.

To locate a person's gravesite –
www.findagrave.com, and see Arlington Cemetery website.

Fort Keogh Post Returns **www.nara.gov** - National Archives and Records Administration 1985, Microfilm Publication, Publication # 666, Roll # 314. Microfilm of hand written reports from Fort Keogh during the Winter Campaign 1876-1877.

About the Author

The author was born and raised in Beardstown, Illinois. Served in Naval Aviation and discharged Viet Nam Vet. 1965.

Lives in Seattle, married, three children, BA from Univ. of Wash., 1974, with duel MBA's from City Univ., 2000.

He became interested in history at a young age, when collecting WWI and II items with his father, J.P. Morgan.

He started reading the Plainsmen Series by the late Terry C. Johnston, which captivated his interest in the Indian Wars. Read extensively and toured Montana, Wyoming, North & South Dakota and Nebraska to locate and walk these sites. The richness for me is the research and then walking these Hallowed Grounds.

Any journey always begins with... the first step!

Printed in the United States
20410LVS00007BA/439-633

This Guide Book was written for those who are interested in touring the battlefields and sites of the American Indian Wars in eastern Montana.

This book provides driving directions using a map, plus GPS coordinates and compass readings for the most advantageous view of these sites.

Each chapter is laid out by the name of the battlefield, fort or cantonment, location, other known names, the campaign name, date(s), principal commanders involved, forces engaged, estimated casualties, a brief history of the battle and the names of Medal of Honor recipients, followed with current pictures of the battlefield. Interesting bits of information, data and observations walked over by the author.

Author has included a copy of the Fort Laramie Treaty of 1868 and a brief on the Indian War Campaign Medal authorized by the Congress 42 years after the Indian campaigns.

Several biographies are included on the officers that served during the Indian campaign, including their continued service and where they are now buried.

The author has included reference books and websites where Indian War Campaigns may be reviewed.

authorHOUSE™